UNDERSTANDING
PHILOSOPHY

MEDIEVAL AND
MODERN PHILOSOPHY

UNDERSTANDING PHILOSOPHY

Ancient and Hellenistic Thought

Medieval and Modern Philosophy

Contemporary Thought

UNDERSTANDING
PHILOSOPHY

MEDIEVAL AND
MODERN PHILOSOPHY

JOAN A. PRICE

CHELSEA HOUSE
PUBLISHERS
An imprint of Infobase Publishing

To my sister, Judy,
for her friendship and love.
❧❧

Medieval and Modern Philosophy

Chelsea House
An imprint of Infobase Publishing
132 West 31st Street
New York NY 10001

Library of Congress Cataloging-in-Publication Data
Price, Joan A.
Medieval and modern philosophy / Joan Price.
    p. cm. -- (Understanding philosophy)
Includes bibliographical references and index.
ISBN 978-0-7910-8740-4 (hardcover)
1. Philosophy, Medieval. 2. Philosophy, Modern. I. Title. II. Series.

B721.P73 2007
190—dc22

Chelsea House books are available at special discounts when purchased in bulk quantities for businesses, associations, institutions, or sales promotions. Please call our Special Sales Department in New York at (212) 967-8800 or (800) 322-8755.

You can find Chelsea House on the World Wide Web at
http://www.chelseahouse.com

Series design by Erika K. Arroyo
Cover design by Ben Peterson

Printed in the United States of America

Bang KT 10 9 8 7 6 5 4 3 2

This book is printed on acid-free paper.

All links and Web addresses were checked and verified to be correct at the time of publication. Because of the dynamic nature of the Web, some address-es and links may have changed since publication and may no longer be valid.

CONTENTS

1

THE MEDIEVAL
PHILOSOPHERS

Disordered love produces a disordered person,
and disordered persons produce a disordered society.
—Saint Augustine

THE ROOTS OF CHRISTIANITY

Christianity grew out of Judaism. It's founder, Jesus Christ, based his teachings on the Jewish faith he was born into. To understand the Christian faith, we need to take a brief look at Jewish history and the Jewish view of God.

Whereas Indo-Europeans (including Greeks and Romans) believed in many different gods, early Jews, or Hebrews, believed in one god who was superior to all other gods, as stated in the Hebrew Bible, Exodus 20:1, 3: "And God spoke these words, saying . . . 'You shall have no other gods before me.'"

The Hebrews believed their god created the entire universe. For them, the world was not eternal, as the Greek philosophers Plato and Aristotle thought, nor did they believe, as did the Stoics, another school of ancient Greek philosophy, the creed, "God in all and all in God." The Hebrews believed God is before the world and transcends the world. The world and everything in it is dependent on God, who is good, righteous, just, and holy. After God created light, the heavens, dry

7

land, vegetation, animals, and human beings, "God saw that it [his creation] was good," in the words of the Hebrew Bible (Genesis 1:25). The Hebrews held a positive attitude about the world and believed the human soul is at home right here on Earth.

Yet, according to the Hebrew Bible, known to Christians as the Old Testament, we cannot always find happiness on Earth because Adam and Eve, the first man and woman, disobeyed God's command in the Garden of Eden. The punishment was a double one: Not only were Adam and Eve banished from the Garden, but death was introduced into the world.

The history as told in the Hebrew Bible concerns the relationship between God and his highest creation: humans. God in the Hebrew Bible is both compassionate and vengeful, punishing those who do wrong or disobey his word. Early in the history of mankind, God brings the Great Flood upon Earth, both as a punishment for the wicked, yet also as redemption for the good—Noah and his family. God later makes a covenant, or agreement, with Abraham in which he promises the Jews protection as his Chosen People if they follow his laws and commandments.

After years of enslavement in Egypt, the Hebrews—with God's help—flee from their bondage back to their homeland in Israel. The Exodus, as the event is called, culminated in God's renewal of his covenant with Abraham, in which Moses was given the Ten Commandments on Mount Sinai in about the year 1200 B.C.

Yet before long, Israel lost its power, and the kingdom was divided into a northern kingdom (Israel) and a southern kingdom (Judea). The Assyrians conquered the northern kingdom, and the Babylonians conquered the southern kingdom and destroyed its temple. Most of the Hebrew people were carried off to Babylon as slaves. Finally, in 539 B.C., the Hebrews returned to Jerusalem, and rebuilt the temple.

In later years, many Jewish prophets preached that God would redeem his people and send them a prince of peace. This Messiah, or Son of God, would restore Israel to greatness and found the Kingdom of God. Some Jews believed that Jesus was the Messiah. In the earliest gospel, meaning "good news," Mark introduces Jesus after his baptism by John, saying, "Now after John was arrested, Jesus came into Galilee, preaching the gospel of God, and saying, 'The time is fulfilled, and the kingdom of God is at hand; repent and believe in the gospel'" (Mark 1:14–15).

Jesus

In the time of Jesus (c. 6 B.C.–A.D. 36), many Jews thought the Messiah would be a political, military, and religious leader who would put an end to their suffering at the hands of their Roman oppressors. Jesus, however, said that he was not a military or political leader. Instead, he preached salvation and God's forgiveness for everyone. He said to the people, "Your sins are forgiven you for his name's sake." Such words shocked the Jews who believed that no one could forgive sins, except God. Jesus also called God "Father," an alien concept to the Jews. They asked who this newcomer, Jesus, was, walking about in sandals and a robe, telling everyone that in the Kingdom of God you must "love thy neighbor as thyself." Jesus also claimed that we must love our enemies. When they strike us, he said, we must turn our other cheek. This was in direct contrast to the Hebrew Bible's belief of "an eye for an eye." Jesus also urges us to forgive: "Love your enemies, do good to those who hate you, bless those who curse you, pray for those who abuse you" (Luke 6:27).

Jesus's words represented a clear break from Jewish thinking and the Hellenistic philosophers of the time. The Jews had not been taught to love their enemies, and Hellenistic schools of philosophy such as the Cynics, Epicureans, and Skeptics all looked for happiness—but not through love of God, because

In the Hebrew Bible, God sends the Great Flood upon Earth to punish mankind for its wickedness, allowing only the righteous Noah and his family to survive. In this fourteenth-century Italian painting, Noah and his family build the ark that God has commanded them to construct.

they did not believe in a personal God, nor did they believe in personal salvation. The Stoics came close to Jesus's teachings in their belief that all humans are brothers and sisters and that we should love our neighbor. Yet, they believed that God was the universe and the universe was God: the Stoic God was not a creator god as was the Jewish and Christian God.

Jesus's message was that "God is love," that he cares for us and will save us from our sinfulness through his son, Jesus, who took our sin upon himself in his death. The heart of his message is in the Gospel of John:

> For God so loved the world that he gave his only Son, that whoever believes in him should not perish but have eternal life. For God sent the Son into the world, not to

condemn the world, but that the world might be saved through him. He who believes in him is not condemned; he who does not believe is condemned already, because he has not believed in the name of the only Son of God. (John 3:16–18).

THE RISE OF CHRISTIANITY

After the Hellenistic era, the period of time roughly from the death of Alexander the Great in 323 B.C. to the conquest of the Greeks by the Romans in 31 B.C., Christianity became the new religion in the Western, or European, world. Although the Hebrew Bible was written in the Semitic family of languages, the Christian New Testament was written in Greek. Therefore, Christian theology and philosophy had close ties with Hellenistic philosophy. Christian philosophers were also theologians, and the main issues concerning them were God, the story of creation, and our human relationship with both. Judaism, Christianity, and Islam are all monotheistic religions, meaning they each believe in one god. That god is omniscient, or all-knowing; omnipotent, or all-powerful; and omnipresent, or being everywhere at the same time. All three religions also believe that, throughout history, God intervenes to reveal his will in the world. One important idea that separates Christianity from Judaism and Islam, however, is its belief in what is called "the Trinity." According to Christian doctrine, God is threefold: Father, Son, and Holy Spirit, or Holy Ghost. Judaism and Islam proclaim, "God is one and only one."

The Hellenistic schools wanted to discover the makeup of human nature through science as well as philosophy, but Christians separated God from science to concentrate on God alone. Hellenistic schools viewed morality as the means to finding self-knowledge and happiness, but Christian moralists relied on the supernatural, and thus looked to God's commands and his judgment of good and evil.

Plato and the Greek Neoplatonists believed humans are innately good but ignorant. Christians believed that humans are born with original sin inherited from Adam and Eve. In general, Christian theologians and philosophers believed that most humans deserved to go to hell, and only God's mercy could save them from such a fate. Gradually, Christianity became such a powerful religion and philosophy that the church itself closed Plato's Academy in Athens, the Western world's first institution of higher learning.

A Brief History of the Church

Christianity had a profound influence on culture and gave its faithful a new lease on life by offering a doctrine of personal salvation. Yet, its influence on the growth of independent philosophical thought during the medieval ages (roughly A.D. 500–1000) was limited because the first Christians held no philosophy of their own. Instead of using reason or dialogue, they relied on their faith in God and in Jesus Christ as the Son of God. They turned from the Greek philosophy of "The unexamined life is not worth living" to "Thus says the Lord!" The key to establishing religious obedience to Christianity was St. Paul's statement in the New Testament, claiming that every soul is subject to the church, which is ordained by God.

During its first 500 years, Christianity became the most powerful religion in Europe via the Catholic Church. The Doctors of the Church—St. Ambrose, St. Jerome, and St. Augustine—developed Christian doctrine and dogma. Through the teachings of Ambrose, the church claimed authority; Jerome translated and edited the New Testament; and Augustine gave Catholicism its doctrinal philosophy.

For 1,000 years, Catholicism influenced the culture of European civilization. The church controlled cultural activities, education, theology, public festivals, and religious ceremonies.

As powerful as the church was in European culture, some kings and emperors rejected its authority. Outside Rome, the heart of the Catholic world, the clergy had to function under the political authority of kings.

During the eleventh century, Pope Gregory VII instituted new church reforms. The priests became more powerful and could determine whether a person would go to heaven or hell. Gregory also introduced celibacy into the priesthood. Before this reform, married priests and bishops who had children could leave their title, lands, and money to their sons. After the reform, everything went to the church. Celibacy also separated the priests from the masses, thus giving them greater respect. Another reform affected the pope, the head of the Roman Catholic Church, and Europe's kings. "The Pope," said Gregory, "is the one representative of God on Earth; he bears the keys to heaven and hell." From then on, a king's authority to rule had to be granted by the pope.

In 1233, Pope Gregory IX founded the Inquisition in response to the growing popularity of heretic creeds, such as the Gnostics and the pagans. Courts of Inquisition were established to judge the guilt of those accused of heresy, a belief in a religion other than that of the church or a denial of the Roman Catholic Church. If those accused of heresy failed to appear before the Inquisition, they were tortured, and if they did not confess to their supposed crime, they were burned at the stake.

As the medieval era drew to a close, the Inquisition tried but failed to stop the Protestant revolution, the rise of science, and advances in philosophy, which announced the dawn of a new era.

EARLY CHRISTIANITY AND PHILOSOPHY

Early Christians considered faith more important than reason or logic, and for that reason philosophy became suspect. Neither Jesus, nor his disciples, were systematic philosophers. In fact, Paul warned the faithful to "beware lest any man spoil you through philosophy and vain deceit." A person must have faith in such revealed truths as the existence of God and that Jesus Christ was the Son of God. Soon, however, the question arose whether Christians must have only faith in the Christian revelation or whether they could also approach Christian revelations with the help of philosophical reasoning.

As more and more educated people flocked to Christianity, they wanted to understand the relationship between the Greek philosophers and the New Testament. Many philosophers and biblical scholars wanted to include rational Greek arguments as a basis for Christian doctrines. In response, some Christian theologians, such as Tertullian, insisted that only faith was important. Reason, he said, has nothing to do with religion: "I believe because it is absurd."

Although many Christian theologians fought the use of Greek philosophy in religion, we can see the influence of Greece and Hellenism in the Gospel of John, which opens by using the Greek word Logos, meaning "word or reason": "In the beginning was the logos and the logos was with God, and the logos was God."

> The influence of Greek philosophy is apparent throughout this gospel, the most popular of the four [Matthew, Mark, and Luke are the other gospels] in Christianity's formative years. . . . Theology, in fact, is not only a Greek word but also an enterprise that is wholly Greek in origin.[1]

Yet, the debate between faith and reason continued throughout the medieval era. St. Augustine and St. Thomas Aquinas, the dominant philosophers and theologians of that time, addressed this question. Augustine based his philosophy and theology on the teachings of Plato and Plotinus. Centuries later, Aquinas looked to Aristotle for the basis of his philosophy. It is a popular saying that Augustine "baptized" Plato into Christianity, and Aquinas "Christianized" Aristotle's philosophy.

Saint Augustine

Augustine believed that God created the world out of nothing and that before God created the world nothing existed. He rejected the Greek idea that the world or matter always existed. Matter is not eternal as the Greeks believed, he said. Augustine did believe, however, that, before God created the world, Plato's Forms were "ideas in the mind of God." Plato's Forms are the true reality—being immaterial and eternal. Augustine, however, rejected Plato's theory of reincarnation and the preexistence of the soul.

Augustine's Life

Aurelius Augustinus, or Augustine (A.D. 354–430), was born in Thagaste, present-day Algeria, in North Africa. His mother was a devout Christian and his father a pagan. At age 17, his parents sent him to Carthage to study rhetoric, the art of speaking persuasively. While there, he found philosophy, rejected Christianity, and took a mistress with whom he had a son. Augustine thought his own sensual desires were evil, and he looked for another religion to explain moral evil and why it exists in people. He also showed concern with the suffering that he saw in the world, asking, "If God is all good, and he created a good world, how is evil possible?" "If God is all-powerful and loving, why do good people suffer?" Christianity's answer didn't satisfy him, so he turned to the Manicheans.

The Manicheans believed there are two basic principles: good and evil. These two principles are eternally in conflict with each other in the world and in us. The conflict exists between the soul, or the good, and the body, or the evil. For

Augustine, this dualism was the reason he could not overcome his sensual desires. The cause of his lust was the power of evil. Shortly, however, Augustine came to the conclusion that a world with two conflicting principles was not logical. Finally, he broke with the Manicheans and joined the thinking of the Skeptics, a group of Greek philosophers from about 200 B.C. who questioned our ability to ever know if there are any absolute truths.

Soon after becoming a Skeptic, Augustine left his mistress to accept teaching positions in Rome and, later, another in Milan. In Milan, he found a new mistress and met Bishop Ambrose, who gave him a fresh appreciation of Christianity. While reading Plotinus's Enneads, Augustine realized how the world could be a unity without two opposing principles. Plotinus, a philosopher from the third century A.D., had turned Augustine to Christianity once again.

Although listening to Bishop Ambrose's sermons and reading Plotinus's works made Christianity more acceptable, Augustine's sensual desires still worried him. To God, he mourned, "Grant me chastity . . . but not yet."

Then, one day while walking in a garden, a child's voice came to him. He looked around, but there was no child. The voice came again, saying, "Read the apostle's book." Augustine obeyed, and his eyes fell on a paragraph: "Not in rioting and drunkenness, not in chambering and wantonness, not in strife and envying, but put on the Lord Jesus Christ, and make not provisions for the flesh." [2]

Augustine's heart filled with light and his doubts vanished. He became baptized, left his mistress, and returned to Africa. There, he founded a monastic community and became a priest two years later. He served the rest of his life as a priest and as bishop of Hippo in Africa. At age 79, Augustine died while reciting the Psalms, as vandals attacked Hippo.

God

Augustine's mystical experience of hearing the voice convinced him we could know certain eternal truths. When he compared his mystical experience with his sensuous desires, he realized that eternal truths gave him an inner peace that his sensual desires could not. Yet, how could he, a finite person, have knowledge of infinite truths? After pondering the question, he came to the conclusion that such knowledge must come from a source greater than himself. That source is God. Without God, who is the source of truth, we could never understand eternal truths. Therefore, God must be present within human beings as well as transcending them. Augustine concluded that such a relation between humans and God could only mean that those who know most about God would come closest to understanding the true nature of the world.

> And how shall I call upon my God, my God and Lord, since, when I call for Him, I shall be calling Him to myself? And what room is there within me, whither my God can come into me? Whither can God come into me, God who made heaven and earth? Is there, indeed, O Lord my God, aught in me that can contain Thee? Do then heaven and earth, which Thou hast made, and wherein Thou hast made me, contain Thee? Or, because nothing which exists could exist without Thee doth therefore whatever exists contain Thee? Since, then, I too exist, why do I seek that Thou shouldest enter into me, who were not, wert Thou not in me? [3]

God's Creation

Augustine believed that God created the world out of nothing. Such an idea was new to Greek and Roman philosophers who believed that you could not get something from nothing. "How could God create a world or anything else out of nothing?" they asked. Augustine rejected Plotinus's theory that all things seek to unify with their source, God. For Augustine, God is utterly distinct from his creation. God created the world from nothing, and before God created the world, nothing existed.

Augustine's Moral Philosophy

Augustine argued that God is good and created the world out of his infinite love. The Creation is an expression of God's goodness. Therefore, God did not create evil. Since God did not create evil, then evil is not a power in itself but an absence of the good. Good is possible without evil, but because "evil is not a power in itself," according to Augustine, evil cannot exist without the good. Evil doesn't spoil the beauty of God's creation because evil is the absence of beauty.

Augustine believed that God could have eliminated evil from the scheme of things, but he saw that it served the good. God gave man free will. Yet, God also knew that human beings, by using their free will, would turn away from the good to evil. By permitting free will, God predetermined human punishment. Evil lies not in ignorance as Plato and Socrates had said, but instead, evil is the result of our own free will. Responsibility for evil lies not with God, but with us.

> It is He who made also man himself upright, with the same freedom of will [as the angels]—an earthly animal, indeed, but fit for heaven if he remained faithful to his Creator, but destined to the misery appropriate to such a nature if he forsook Him. It is He who, when He foreknew that man would in his turn sin by abandoning God and breaking His law, did not deprive him of the power of free-will, because He at the same

time foresaw what good He Himself would bring out of the evil.[4]

Augustine believed that every human being inherited original sin from the Fall of Adam and Eve. The cause of the fall was pride. Adam and Eve had tried to become like God, to be self-sufficient. In trying to rise above their proper place in the chain of being, the first humans fell. "Pride is the start of every kind of sin" (Proverbs 16:18). From pride comes moral evil and turning away from God. "This then," said Augustine, "is the original evil: man regards himself as his own light." Humans also have free will to turn toward God by choosing the good. Yet, although we can choose the good life, we do not have the spiritual power to actually live the good life. To make his point, Augustine often quoted a passage from St. Paul:

> I do not understand my own actions. For I do not do what I want, but I do the very thing I hate. . . . I can will what is right, but I cannot do it. For I do not do the good I want, but the evil I do not want is what I do. Now if I do what I do not want, it is no longer I that do it, but sin which dwells within me. (Romans 7:15, 18–20)

Since we cannot live the good life by our own efforts, only by God's grace are we free to obey him to achieve moral goodness. No human really deserves salvation, said Augustine, yet God has graciously chosen to save some people, but not all, from damnation. Only God's grace can lead a person to salvation. Our destiny is entirely at God's mercy.

> That the whole human race has been condemned in its first origin, this life itself, if life it is to be called, bears witness by the host of cruel ills with which it is felled. Is

not this proved by the profound and dreadful ignorance which produces all the errors that enfold the children of Adam, and from which no man can be delivered without toil, pain, and fear? Is it not proved by his love of so many vain and hurtful things, which produces gnawing cares, disquiet, griefs, fears, wild joys, quarrels, law-suits, wars, treasons, angers, hatreds, deceit, flattery, fraud, theft, robbery, perfidy, pride, ambition, envy, murders, parricides, cruelty, ferocity, wickedness, luxury, insolence, impudence, shamelessness, fornications, adulteries, incests, and the numberless uncleannesses and unnatural acts of both sexes. . . . These error and misplaced love which is born with every son of Adam. . . . From this hell upon earth there is no escape, save through the grace of the Saviour Christ, our God and Lord. [5]

The Role of Love

Augustine agreed with Aristotle that all humans seek happiness, but he did not agree with Aristotle that we could find happiness by satisfying our "natural" functions. For Aristotle, we could satisfy our natural functions by living a well-balanced life. Not so, said Augustine. God created us, and, therefore, we have to go beyond the natural to the "supernatural" to find happiness. God is love and he created humans to love. In this world, all things are worthy of love. We can love physical objects, other persons, and even ourselves. Love of these things can provide us with some measure of satisfaction and happiness. Our problems lie in the way we love those things.

Often, we expect too much from what we love, leading to what Augustine says is "disordered love." For example, we may believe that a larger television, a faster car, or fashionable clothes would make us happy. Yet, physical objects do not last, and excessive love of them leads to the sin of greed.

Have you ever thought that you would be happy if a particular person loved you? The truth is, other people cannot provide us with lasting happiness. They die, or leave us, or fail to live up to our expectations. Furthermore, too much love of another person can lead to the sin of jealousy.

St. Augustine believed that people have free will and decide their own destiny, but that God knows what we will decide. He also believed that, if we choose the good, we do not have the will to follow it entirely, and we need God's grace to lead us to salvation.

Loving ourselves is important. Jesus said, "Love your neighbor as yourself." Yet, the wrong kind of self-love, such as, "I am a better baseball player than anyone else on the team," or, "I'm the smartest person in my class," leads to pride. For Augustine, pride is the root of all sin, including the Fall of Adam and Eve.

Although all things are worthy of love, only by loving God do we find true happiness. For Augustine, love of God is not temporary, nor does it lead to sin. In order to love physical objects, other people, and ourselves properly, we must love God first.

Augustine's Two Cities

In his book *The City of God*, Augustine divided humanity into two groups: those who love God and those who turn away from God to love themselves and the world. Since there are two opposing loves, then there are two opposing societies: the City of God and the City of the World. Those who belong to the City of God realize that the only eternal good is in God, and those in the City of the World seek the good in themselves and the world. Augustine did not identify the church and the state as the two cities because those who love the world are found in both the church and the world, as are those who love God. For Augustine, the difference is that between "disordered love," or worldly love, and "ordered love," or the love of God.

> Accordingly, two cities have been formed by two loves, the earthly by love of self, even to the contempt of God: the heavenly by the love of God, even to the contempt of self. The former, in a word, glorifies itself, the latter in the Lord. For the one seeks glory from man; but the greatest glory of the other is God, the witness of conscience. The one lifts up its head in its own glory; the other says to its God, Thou art my glory, and the lifter up of mine head.[6]

Saintly Christians who live in the City of the World are actually citizens of the City of God. They live in the world but are not of the world. In the City of the World, these Christians obey the laws of the state, yet they serve and love God above all.

Augustine's View of History

Before Augustine, the Greeks had viewed history as cyclic, meaning that civilizations rise and fall, and then new civilizations are born. Augustine, however, viewed history as linear. He claimed that the world began with the Creation, and it will end with the destruction of the world as we know it. Until that time, history is the struggle between the City of God and the City of the World. Ultimately, the City of God will triumph.

History, said Augustine, is the unfolding of God's plan for his creation. God needs history to realize his Kingdom of God on Earth. Therefore, history is necessary for the spiritual life of human beings and the destruction of the City of the World. Augustine believed that God directs the history of humankind from Adam to the end of time.

According to Augustine, the role of the Catholic Church in history is to control the sinful nature of human beings. Yet, God will not save everyone within the church because some individuals in the church have their hearts and minds in the City of the World, and God will not save anyone who is outside the church.

THE DARK AGES

The Dark Ages refers to the medieval period of intellectual darkness in Europe that occurred after the fall of the Roman Empire in A.D. 476. During this time, learning almost came to a halt. For the next five centuries, Christian scholars were found mostly in monasteries where they copied important Greek manuscripts and wrote books. In the ninth century, King Charlemagne, the ruler of western and central Europe, tried to revive public education, but with the fall of his family's Carolinian Empire, education plunged deeper into decline. Finally, in the last half of the eleventh century, intellectual activity began to take hold, and universities developed as major centers of learning. During the Dark Ages, however, university philosophers and theologians continued to tackle three touchy problems: (1) faith and reason, (2) integrating Greek philosophy with the teachings of Christianity, and (3) proving the existence of God through reason.

Faith Versus Reason

Medieval theologians believed that, because so few individuals receive God's revelation, people should have faith in the authority of those who had experienced it. Yet, some scholars asked, "What if revelations contradict one another?" Today, for example, the revelations of the president of the Mormon Church contradict the revelations received by authorities in the Catholic Church. Medieval scholars also questioned reason: "How can we depend on reason to answer our questions about God when philosophers themselves disagree with each other?" For example, Aristotle's theory of God differed from Plotinus's theory of God, and Augustine's theory of God differed from both. Medieval Christian scholars were in turmoil and struggled to find answers to such questions.

MUSLIM PHILOSOPHY

The Muslim religion, known as Islam, began with the Prophet Muhammad (570–632), an Arab from the city of Mecca in what is now Saudi Arabia. Allah, the Muslim name for God, commanded Muhammad to cast out polytheism, or the belief in many gods, and to teach people that "there is no God but Allah." Over a 23-year period, Muhammad received messages from Allah. Muhammad memorized the messages, and his disciples wrote them down in a work known as the Qur'an, or Koran. These sacred writings taught a message of submission to the will of Allah. The word Islam means "submission."

After Muhammad established a vast Muslim empire with cultural centers in Persia and Spain, important philosophical activity began to take place. During the ninth through the twelfth centuries, the Muslim world was far more advanced in philosophy, science, and mathematics than was the Christian world. Arab philosophers Avicenna and Averroes had the works of Aristotle available to them long before western Europe received them. The interpretations of Aristotle by these two significant philosophers influenced many Christian and Jewish writers.

Avicenna

Avicenna (980–1037) was born in Persia (present-day Iran) and grew up studying philosophy, mathematics, science, and medicine, all of which he mastered by age 18. As an adult, he practiced medicine and wrote more than 100 works on philosophy, science, and religion. Avicenna's book *The Canon of Medicine* was used in medical schools of medieval universities, and his philosophical writings influenced future medieval philosophy. In his life as a doctor and high government official, he managed to find time to write 160 books on a wide range of subjects.

The thinking of Aristotle and Neoplatonism were both important parts of Avicenna's philosophical system. Considered one of the most brilliant philosophers of the medieval world, Avicenna expressed the difficulties of Aristotle's writings when he said, "I have read his metaphysics forty times and I think I am beginning to understand it."

God

Avicenna is especially remembered for his doctrine of creation. Unlike Augustine, who said that God freely chose to create the world, Avicenna saw Allah as a necessary being who emanated, or created, the world out of himself as a result of his self-knowledge. Avicenna referred to God as the First Cause and prime mover, who is eternal and always in the act of emanating. The first emanation is intelligence, and intelligence repeatedly creates a lesser intelligence for ten more levels. The tenth intelligence, which is the equivalent to what Aristotle called the "Active Intellect," creates human souls and the four elements of the world—earth, air, fire, and water. Human souls differ from the Active Intellect because they contain matter.

The Soul

The human soul has rational knowledge that was emanated from the Active Intellect, but it also has an irrational nature that is matter. Unlike Plato, who said the soul preexists, Avicenna believed the soul is created when the body is created. At death, however, the soul separates from the body to exist eternally as an individual. The souls of persons who have led pure lives enter eternal bliss, but impure souls experience eternal torment, seeking their lost bodies. Avicenna referred to the soul as individual—the "I" that is permanent throughout all bodily change. The goal of the soul is to attain intuitive knowledge of Allah and his creation.

JEWISH PHILOSOPHY

From the ninth through the twelfth centuries, both Muslim and Jewish philosophy was more advanced than Christian philosophy. The reason was that Christian philosophers did not have access to Aristotle's texts. The great Jewish philosopher Maimonides became familiar with the works of Aristotle through Muslim philosophers. Both Muslim and Jewish philosophers would have a powerful influence on the Christian philosophy of the next century.

Moses Maimonides

Moses ben Maimonides (1135–1204) was born in Cordova, Spain. As a boy, his father tutored him in the Bible, the Talmud, and science. At age 13, Muslims from North Africa conquered his city and closed its synagogues. The Muslims gave the Jewish community three options: conversion to Islam, death, or exile. Maimonides's family chose exile and moved first to Morocco and then to Cairo, Egypt. There, Maimonides and his brother, David, became jewel merchants. A few years later, Maimonides lost both his father and David, the latter killed in a shipwreck in the Indian Ocean during a business trip. Maimonides gave up the jewel business, attended medical school, and became a physician. His excellence as a doctor led to his appointment as a court physician for the Arab ruler Saladin, who defeated Richard the Lionheart in the Third Crusade. Maimonides's deep spirituality led his peers to elect him the spiritual head of the Egyptian Jewish community. Following his death at age 69, his body was taken from Cairo to Tiberias on the Sea of Galilee. In reverence to his life and work, people today still visit his tomb.

Maimonides especially influenced Christian thinkers because he shared with them knowledge of the Hebrew Bible as well as the philosophy of Aristotle. His writings served as a model for Thomas Aquinas on such issues as faith and reason.

Faith and Reason

Maimonides's book *The Guide for the Perplexed* brings together both Jewish religious law and Greek philosophy. In it, Maimonides demonstrated that no conflict really exists between theology, philosophy, and science. Nor, he said, does there need to be a conflict between faith and reason. The counterpart of rational virtue is in faith, thus both faith and reason are necessary. Maimonides agreed with Aristotle that we could prove the existence of God by using reason. He said that biblical prophecy is a continuing flow of reason and inspiration from God to our human mind:

> I will mention to you, as an instance, man's reason, which being one faculty and implying no plurality, enables him to know many arts and sciences; by the same faculty man is able to sow, to do carpenter's work, to weave, to build, to study, to acquire a knowledge of geometry, and to govern a state. These various acts resulting from one simple faculty, which involves no plurality, are very numerous; their number, that is, the number of actions originating in man's reason, is almost infinite. It is therefore intelligible how in reference to God, those different actions can be caused by one simple substance [reason] that does not include any plurality or any additional element. [7]

Maimonides believed that the highest human perfection is acquiring rational virtues. As seen through the inspiration of the Prophets, there is also virtue in faith. Thus, reason and faith together are the ultimate virtue.

God

For Maimonides, God is one eternal spirit without any finite human traits. When reading the Bible, people should understand that terms used to describe God are allegorical, because no language can explain the infinite nature of God. Only by negation (God is not this, God is not that) of our finite characteristics could we have any insight into God.

A HIGH POINT FOR CHRISTIANITY

In the early part of the medieval ages, most philosophers and theologians considered Augustine the authority of church philosophy. Augustine had combined the Christian faith with much of Plato's thought, which he had discovered in the writings of Plotinus. In the thirteenth century, Thomas Aquinas challenged Augustine by bringing Aristotle's philosophy into Christianity and giving a rational proof of God's existence.

Although some of Aristotle's works had been available to western Europeans, his most important writings were found only in the Islamic world. By 1250, all of his works had been introduced to the West, with commentaries written by Muslim and Jewish philosophers. The effect of Aristotle on Christian thinking was to change spiritual and intellectual life throughout the West. Aristotle provided the tools of reasoning to support Christian teachings, introducing scientific ideas to medieval thinking. Yet, problems arose concerning his works. First, Aristotle did not believe in a creator god because he believed that the world is eternal, with no beginning or end. Thus, it was not created. Second, he denied personal salvation, and third, Aristotle's God was not interested in the world of everyday affairs. The way Aquinas dealt with these problems was a new high point in Christianity.

St. Thomas Aquinas

In his book *History of Philosophy* Martyn Oliver sums up the impact of St. Thomas Aquinas on the thinking of his time:

> The work of Thomas Aquinas is the chief source of modern Catholic theology. His writing was part of a cultural revolution in Europe in the 13th century. Universities were established all over Europe and the teaching of the seven liberal arts (grammar, logic, rhetoric, arithmetic, geometry, music and astronomy) was received by increasing numbers of students. This expansion of the scholarly world helped create

an atmosphere in which the received doctrines of the Catholic Church, founded upon the theology of Augustine, were challenged. Aquinas challenged dominant Catholic theology by embracing writings derived from the re-appraisal of ancient scholarship. [8]

Aquinas's Life

Thomas Aquinas (1225–1274) was born in Aquino, near Naples in southern Italy. His father was a count of Aquino who wanted his son to someday enjoy a high position in the church. Thus, at age five, Aquinas was sent to the Monte Cassino to pursue his studies in the Benedictine abbey. When Thomas was 14, a serious political disagreement between the church and the Holy Roman emperor made the monastery unsafe. His parents sent him to the University of Naples.

While Aquinas was at the university, his father died. That same year, Aquinas shocked the rest of his family by deciding to join the Dominican Order and live in poverty. His family was so upset by his decision that they kidnapped him and held him captive in the family castle for a year. They tried everything to change his mind, even tempting him with a prostitute, but Aquinas stood firm. Realizing he would never change his mind, his family finally released him to become a Dominican friar.

Four years after he became a friar, Aquinas went to Paris to study with Albertus Magnus, or Albert the Great, an admirer of Aristotle. A story about Aquinas developed: Because he was so methodical in everything he did and had a heavy build, his peers dubbed him "the Dumb Ox." But Albertus rebuffed them, saying, "You call him a Dumb Ox; I tell you the Dumb Ox will bellow so loud his bellowing will fill the world." In 1256, Aquinas received his doctorate degree in theology from the University of Paris and was asked to join the university faculty.

Called from the university, he taught for the next nine years under the sponsorship of the papal courts before returning to Paris. Aquinas wrote more than 20 volumes. Yet, as a result of

St. Thomas Aquinas is considered by many to be the Catholic Church's leading theologian. Aquinas believed that the goal of human life is to unite into eternal fellowship with God.

a profound mystical experience in December 1273, he stopped writing. After the experience, he said to a friend, "All I have written seems like straw to me." The next year, Pope Gregory X asked Aquinas to attend a general council in Lyons, France, but on his way to the meeting, Aquinas became ill and died. He was 49. In 1332, the church canonized him as St. Thomas Aquinas.

Faith and Reason

Unlike some other medieval philosophers, Aquinas saw no conflict between philosophical reasoning and faith based on Christian revelation. He agreed that we cannot know God through reason alone, but through faith and reason together we could reach "natural theological truth." Aquinas believed the concept that "there is a God" is a truth we can trust through both faith and reason. Theology, he said, always begins with faith in God. Reason begins with sense experience and proceeds step-by-step toward God. Faith is based on direct revelation that comes directly from God. So, although faith and reason use different methods, they don't contradict each other. To make his point, Aquinas set out to prove God's existence by the use of reason.

Five Proofs for the Existence of God

Believing that God exists is a condition of faith. By using reason, however, Aquinas devised five proofs to demonstrate the truth of God's existence. He began by pointing out that knowledge begins with our experience of sense objects. Reason innately knows that each object we experience has a cause, or an origin. Reason also knows that every effect must have a cause, and so there must ultimately be a "First Cause" of everything. Aquinas called this First Cause God. He came to this conclusion by reason, not by faith.

Briefly, Aquinas's "five ways" to prove the existence of God are

1. *Proof from motion.* We can see that all things in the natural world are moving. It follows that something must have put everything in motion, namely, a First Mover of all motion. That First Mover is God.

2. *Proof from efficient cause.* Nothing in our world causes itself. You did not cause yourself, nor did a statue cause itself. Thus, everything is the effect of some cause other than itself. There had to be a First Cause of everything (much like Aristotle's Efficient Cause theory). That First Cause is God.

3. *Proof from necessary versus possible being.* In nature, it is possible for some things not to exist, such as you and I. Before we were born, we did not exist. Now we exist, and then we will die. There must be something that not just possibly exists but necessarily exists as the cause of all "possible beings." That necessary being is God.

4. *Proof from the degrees of perfection.* In this world, we view some things as better than others. Some people are less good and less truthful than others. There also are various degrees of beauty. Thus, we must have some standard ideal of the highest Goodness, Truth, and Beauty. We also compare lesser and higher beings. A monkey is a higher being than a rock, and a human is a higher being than a monkey. From this, Aquinas concluded there must be something perfect to cause all the degrees of perfection. That perfect being is God.

5. *Proof from the order and design of the universe.* Everything in nature has a purpose and seeks certain ends. The acorn grows into an oak tree, never a carrot. The girl becomes a woman, never a fish. Every year we have autumn, winter, spring, and summer. Where there is order and design, there is an intelligent mind responsible for that order and design. That intelligent mind is God.

For Aquinas, the five proofs show that we can prove God's existence by using reason. These are proofs, he said, that all rational people could agree upon. Although the five proofs prove God's existence, the full truth of God can only be known through revelation based on grace, or having a profound mystical experience.

Evil

For Aquinas, God is all-good, all-knowing, and all-powerful. The question arises, "If God is all-good and all-powerful, how can there be evil in the world?" Aquinas tackled this problem by saying that God created the universe to communicate his love. Thus, God is not responsible for evil. Like Plato, Plotinus, and Augustine, Aquinas believed evil is not a force in itself but the absence of good. He also accepted Augustine's belief that evil is a product of our free will. Yet, he disagreed with Augustine that if we knew the good we would still choose to do evil. He agreed with Socrates and Plato that no one would intentionally choose to do evil just because it is evil. An adulterer does not choose to do evil; he or she chooses an act that brings pleasure. Such pleasure, said Aquinas, lacks goodness and is therefore evil.

In his love, God willed human beings the freedom to choose good or evil. If we could choose only the good, then we would not be free. But why would an all-loving God allow suffering in nature, such as a child born with a crippling disease? Aquinas answered that God did not will suffering in itself. He only willed a natural order that allowed for physical defects and suffering.

Thomas [Aquinas's] intellect was of the same rank as Plato's and Aristotle's; with him we reach another philosophical mountain peak. Indeed, he stands functionally to the Middle Ages as Plato and Aristotle do to the classical world. Like them, he gave a definitive answer to the major intellectual problems of his times. What were the problems that Thomas set himself to solve? ... They were in part, purely dogmatic, that is, they were problems related to the old task of working out a consistent theology. [9]

Aquinas's Moral Philosophy

Like Aristotle, Aquinas thought that morality is rational. By using reason, we can know how we should behave. Of course, we must live according to God's intentions, which means we must be honest, keep our promises, and refrain from greed and other sins. Reason tells us what choices we should make, and God gave us the freedom to make those choices. Like Aristotle before him, Aquinas viewed virtue as a mean between the two extremes of "too much" or "too little." Making the right choices means finding the mean between these extremes. We will be virtuous when reason controls our sensuous appetites.

Sin

Aquinas identified two types of sin: venial sin and mortal sin. Venial sins, such as disrespecting your parents, are pardonable because we can make amends. Mortal sins, such as stealing or murder, however, harm the soul and they are unpardonable. Aquinas also described three kinds of virtue: theological, moral, and intellectual. Theological virtues are faith, hope, and love, and are given to us by God. Moral virtues consist of self-control, courage, and justice. Intellectual virtues consist of wisdom and understanding. All of these virtues will lead us to find happiness in God.

LINKS TO MODERN PHILOSOPHY

In the medieval world, philosophy and theology concentrated on understanding God through faith or reason (or both) with a view to human salvation. For hundreds of years, medieval philosophers and theologians ignored science because they preferred to focus on God. Gradually, however, philosophers and scientists shifted their interests to the natural world to free themselves from fixed church doctrines. The era of modern philosophy was about to begin—a time of philosophical and scientific discovery and a whole new way of looking at things.

2

THE BIRTH OF MODERN PHILOSOPHY
The Renaissance Period

All noble things are as difficult as they are rare.
—Benedict de Spinoza

THE RENAISSANCE PERIOD

The late fourteenth century was the beginning of the Renaissance, a French word meaning "rebirth," a period of rich cultural development and a new way of viewing human nature. The movement began in northern Italy and spread rapidly northward during the fifteenth and sixteenth centuries. Lasting through the seventeenth century, the Renaissance was a rebirth in attitudes in which human beings were viewed as noble and worthy rather than merely sinful creatures. The concept of rebirth was also expressed in the art and culture of ancient times. The ideal person in this era was the Renaissance man, a person of universal genius in life as well as in the arts, literature, and science.

In the medieval era, philosophers viewed God as separate from his creation. According to this thinking, nature is not divine or sacred. Renaissance humanist Giordano Bruno, however, saw God as being present in his creation. Bruno, like the Greek Stoics, was a pantheist, or one who sees God in all things; he believed that nature was divine and sacred. The Catholic Church condemned Bruno as a pagan heretic and burned him at the stake.

Gradually, however, just as Greek philosophy broke away from ancient mythologies, the Renaissance middle class began to break away from the feudal lords and the power of the Roman Catholic Church. During the Renaissance, church and state authorities conducted witch trials, burned heretics, condemned magic, and waged bloody religious wars. Such harsh acts, however, could not stop the new thinking of philosophers and scientists about the nature of human beings and the world.

Martin Luther

During the fourteenth and fifteenth centuries, the Christian papacy, the system of government of the Roman Catholic Church, was in constant turmoil. Both the bishop of Rome, Italy, and the bishop of Avignon, France, claimed the title of pope. In fact, each one excommunicated the other. Eventually, the bishop of Rome became the only pope. About this same time, some Roman Catholics expressed concern about the excesses and abuses they saw within their church. One of them, a Catholic monk named Martin Luther, decided to challenge the church's actions.

Luther's Life and Church Reforms

Martin Luther (1483–1546) was the son of Hans Luder, a copper-mining businessman. Luder was a stern man who often fought with his son. Martin attended school in Mansfeld, Germany, but when the family moved to Magdeburg, he was enrolled in the cathedral school. There, he joined friends who belonged to a spiritual group called the Brethren of the Common Life. At age 18, he attended the University of Erfurt, where he completed his undergraduate work and a master's degree. Following graduation, Luther studied law to please his father, but after a profound spiritual experience, he left law to become a monk. Two years later, he was ordained to the Roman Catholic priesthood.

In 1509, Luther returned to Erfurt to study theology. While there, he joined the Augustinian order, which was based on the teachings of St. Augustine, and they sent him to Rome on business. Luther had thought of Rome as the center of the church and a highly spiritual place, but he was disappointed because his impression of the city was that it was too worldly. After his return to Erfurt, he transferred to a monastery in Wittenberg where he completed his doctorate in theology. Later, he became a professor of biblical theology at the University of Wittenberg.

Throughout the years, Luther became more and more disillusioned with church authority. Finally, on October 31, 1517, he posted sheets of paper containing 95 theses to the chapel door at the University of Wittenberg, boldly challenging many Catholic doctrines and practices.

Luther believed that each person was responsible for living a good life and should not be dependent on church authority. He criticized the church's practice of selling indulgences, which were guarantees of receiving forgiveness of one's sins with no punishment in purgatory. You cannot buy your way to salvation, Luther said, because salvation comes only from God's grace. Luther also criticized the pope's control of the treasury of merits, which were indulgences given to the faithful out of which the pope could, in Luther's words, "draw credits" for himself. Luther also strongly criticized the pope's pride:

> The Pope is not satisfied with riding on horseback or in a carriage, but though he be hale and strong, is carried by men like an idol in unheard-of pomp. My friend, how does this Lucifer-like pride agree with the example of Christ, who went on foot, as did also all the Apostles? [10]

This engraving shows Martin Luther having just nailed his 95 Theses to the door of Castle Church in Wittenberg, Germany, in 1517. Luther's challenges to the Catholic Church sparked a theological debate that resulted in the Protestant Reformation.

Luther also spoke out against the doctrine of purgatory, the monastic life, and the church's preoccupation with money concerns during the Mass.

Luther wanted Christianity to be as he found it in the New Testament. He thought that everyone should read the Bible and communicate with God in his own way without the intercession of a priest. When Luther refused to apologize for his statements, the pope excommunicated him, throwing Luther out of the church and condemning him to hell. Fortunately, a friendly duke offered him refuge in his castle, where Luther spent his days translating the Greek Bible into German. For the first time in history, the Bible could be read in the German language.

Luther considered Saint Augustine to be his spiritual teacher and, like Augustine, he believed that humans became totally corrupt after the Fall of Adam and Eve and that personal salvation could only come through the grace of God.

Luther married a former nun, and they had several children. According to Luther, a woman's place was not in the church but in the home raising the family. He died in Eisleben, the city of his birth, at age 63.

THE PROTESTANT REFORMATION

Luther's protests and desire for reform started the famous historical movement known as the Protestant Reformation. The word protestant means "to protest."

Disgusted with the corruption among the clergy, many Christians applauded Luther's proposed reforms. When Luther left the church, thousands of monks, priests, and nuns left their monasteries and convents to join the Reformation. The ruling royal classes across Europe were also anxious to eliminate or weaken the pope's power over their subjects. Luther's ideas quickly took root, especially in Germany and Scandinavia.

The Protestant Reformation had a strong influence on philosophy, particularly ethics. No longer did philosophers believe that moral practices depended upon priestly authority or the dogma of the church. Instead, the Reformation steered people to look within themselves for the answers to moral virtue.

THE RISE OF SCIENCE

Throughout the medieval ages, Christian philosophers and theologians had little use for science and scientific theory. For instance, because the Bible said that God created man in his image, church authorities taught that our Earth was the center of the universe. Most people believed that Earth remained still while the heavenly bodies in space traveled in their orbits around it. They also believed that God ruled from high above all the heavenly bodies.

Nicholaus Copernicus

In 1543, however, in a book entitled *On the Revolutions of Heavenly Bodies*, a shocking theory was postulated by author Nicholaus Copernicus (1473–1543). Born in present-day Poland, Copernicus was a mathematician, astronomer, physician, and government and military leader. In his book, Copernicus claimed that the Sun did not revolve around Earth but that Earth and other planets revolved around the Sun. His stunning hypothesis, however, had to wait a century to be proved.

Galileo Galilei

Galileo Galilei (1564–1642), an Italian physicist and astronomer, was the one to finally support Copernicus's claims; Galileo discovered moons circling Jupiter, confirming that Earth was not the center of the universe. Using his telescope to observe, he studied the Moon's craters and said that the Moon had mountains and valleys similar to those on Earth. Although Galileo was a Catholic, church officials were made uneasy by his claims, and they summoned him to face a council of Inquisition in Rome for heresy. In 1633, the council forced Galileo to reject his findings by threatening him with excommunication. Disturbed with the prospect of excommunication, Galileo agreed to the council's demands. He renounced his findings to the council, but as he was leaving the room, he whispered, "I recant, but nonetheless my findings are true." For the rest of his life, he was under house arrest. Recognized as a scientific genius by the rest of the world, Galileo was not acknowledged by the Roman Catholic Church for 300 years. Finally, in 1992, the church restored his good name and reputation.

For hundreds of years, the Roman Catholic Church placed *On the Revolutions of Heavenly Bodies* on its Index of Forbidden Books. Copernicus's theory fared no better with Martin Luther and other Protestant leaders who believed his teachings contradicted several Old Testament claims.

Isaac Newton

Despite disapproval from Christian leaders, a scientific method of investigation began to flourish throughout Europe. Dutch scientist Anton van Leeuwenhoek discovered the circulation of blood in the human body. Englishman Robert Boyle, the father of chemistry, devised a formula on the relation of temperature, volume, and pressure of gases. Both English physicist Sir Isaac Newton and German philosopher Baron Gottfried Wilhelm von Leibniz, working independently, invented the differential and integral calculus.

Newton (1643–1727) also described the solar system and the planetary orbits. He not only explained that the planets moved around the Sun but also how these bodies in motion behaved. One day, while Newton was sitting under an apple tree, an apple fell on his head. From this "Aha!" experience, he formulated his law of universal gravitation, commonly known as the law of gravity.

By discovering the law of gravity, Newton eliminated the medieval belief that there is one set of laws for heaven and another for Earth. Astronomers were convinced that there was no absolute center to the universe. They believed there were just as many centers as there were people. Each person could be the center of a universe.

Thomas Hobbes

Instead of looking to church authority for the truth, these scientists and philosophers looked to nature for the truth. One of their major interests was to explain the human condition and the nature of society. Thomas Hobbes, a famous English philosopher of the seventeenth century, called the relationship between people and their society a "social contract."

Hobbes's Life

Thomas Hobbes (1588–1679) was born in Westport, England, and educated at Oxford University. There, he found Aristotle's logic boring and instead turned to classical literature. After graduation, Hobbes became the tutor for the son of the Cavendish family. This association allowed him to travel and meet leading thinkers of the day. When he was 40, Hobbes discovered Euclid's Elements. Written by the Greek mathematician Euclid in about 300 B.C., the book excited Hobbes because in it he saw geometry as the key to understanding nature:

> Being in a gentleman's library, Euclid's *Elements* lay open, and 'twas the 47th [theorem of Book 1]. He read the proposition. "By God," said he, "this is impossible . . ." So he reads the demonstration of it, which referred him back to such a proposition: which proposition he read. That referred him back to another, which he also read . . .

at last he was demonstratively convinced of that truth. This made him in love with geometry. [11]

Hobbes was a materialist, someone who believes that all things come from concrete physical substances. Materialism is the opposite of idealism. Philosophers of idealism believe that what exists in nature is in essence spiritual, not material. Hobbes agreed with the Greek pre-Socratic philosopher Democritus who said that everything, including humans, consists of particles of matter. Even the human soul develops from the movement of tiny particles in the brain, Democritus claimed. Because the mechanical laws of nature govern everything, said Hobbes, it is possible to calculate every natural change with mathematical precision.

Social Contract

Hobbes believed that people are basically self-centered and selfish. They look to their own security before anything else. People are, he said, competitive, selfish, violent, and in need of security. They identify goodness with the satisfaction of their own selfish desires. To control their selfishness, people form societies in which they agree to surrender authority to a ruler who keeps them in check. Therefore, society is a compromise, a "social contract" in which people are willing to give up their individual freedom for security and cooperation. Because the ruler has the power to judge what is best for the people, the state has control over religion.

As a materialist, Hobbes believed that everything, including human beings, is matter and has no spiritual qualities. His conclusions that humans were amoral with no inner sense of right and wrong offended Catholics and Protestants alike. Yet, the boldness of his ideas challenged philosophers and scientists to find a more positive and encouraging view of the world and human life.

THE CONTINENTAL RATIONALISTS

Like Socrates and Plato, the Continental rationalists of Europe thought we could discover the truth by using reason. For these philosophers, the rational mind is the only path to knowledge, and we can conduct our own lives without looking to church authority for answers. By using reason, these philosophers wanted to give philosophy the exactness of mathematics. Three of the most notable Continental rationalists were René Descartes, who described reality as two separate substances, namely, "mind and matter"; Benedict de Spinoza, who viewed reality as a single substance with "attributes and modes"; and Gottfried Wilhelm Leibniz, who called the basic substance a "windowless monad."

René Descartes

Known as the father of modern philosophy and the father of modern mathematics, Descartes was the first to construct an entirely new system of philosophy from the ground up. His main concern was with what we can know. The other great question that fascinated him was the relationship between mind and body. These questions would be the core of philosophical investigations for the next 150 years.

Descartes's Life

René Descartes (1596–1650), the son of a noble family, was born at La Haye, Tourain, France. Soon after Descartes's birth, his mother died. For most of his life, his own health was frail. A brilliant boy, at age eight, his father enrolled him in the Royal Jesuit College of La Flèche. Because of his fragile health, the Jesuit teachers allowed him to stay in bed in the morning and attend classes in the afternoon. At school, Descartes found that the infallibility of mathematics solved all his doubts about certainty. To Descartes, whether a person lived in Europe or in India, or whether they studied Plato or Hobbes, or whether they were religious or not, it was the preciseness of mathematics that could answer all questions.

After college graduation, Descartes's father left him an inheritance that allowed him to travel throughout Europe. He lived in Paris but found its social life boring, and he hid from his friends to study alone. Finally, he left Paris and attended the University of Poitiers to study law. After receiving his degree, he joined the army as a gentleman volunteer. While in the army, Descartes had time to meditate on his idea of connecting mathematical certainty with philosophy. A story is told that Descartes, preferring warmth to cold, crawled into a huge Bavarian oven—not in use at the time—to meditate on his ideas. When he came out of the oven that evening, he said to his associates that his philosophy was half-finished. Those who did not agree with Descartes's theories jokingly said his philosophy was half-baked.

After his army service, Descartes moved to Holland where he spent the next 20 years writing and publishing his ideas. In 1649, Queen Christina of Sweden invited him to Stockholm to give her philosophy lessons. He politely refused her twice. The third time, she sent a warship to take him to the "land of bears, ice, and rocks," as he called her kingdom. Once there, Descartes discovered that the only time Queen Christina had for her lessons was at 5:00 A.M., in her cold, damp castle. Within a few months, Descartes caught pneumonia and died. He was 54.

Descartes introduced mathematical concepts known as Cartesian coordinates and curves, and he also invented analytic geometry. A Roman Catholic, Descartes wanted to reconcile church teachings with the new science, but the church placed his writings on the Index of Forbidden Books. Yet, the Catholic Church was not alone, and even Protestant theologians attacked Descartes's writings.

The Cartesian Method

The word Cartesian comes from the Latin form of Descartes's name, Renatus Cartesius. Descartes's method of inquiry began when he asked, "What, if anything, can I know with certainty?" To find an answer, he looked to literature, poetry, theology, philosophy, and finally to the "book of the world," that is, the experiences and wisdom of ordinary people. Yet, he found just as many differences of opinion among these people as among

This detail of an eighteenth-century painting shows René Descartes (standing, pointing to papers) giving a lecture on geometry to Queen Christina of Sweden (in blue dress). Descartes's development of Cartesian geometry is still taught today.

the other disciplines. Then, one night, he had three dreams that were so vivid he was sure God had sent them. The dreams told him to develop his own system of knowledge, using the powers of human reason alone.

As Descartes reflected on the human reason, he discovered that the mind has two powers: (1) intuition, which is direct and clear insight into basic truths, and (2) deduction, which is the mind's ability to arrive at a truth by a step-by-step procedure. He decided to use intuition and deduction to test the validity of his findings and to reject anything that did not pass the test of these two faculties.

Descartes's Method of Doubt

Descartes decided that the first thing to be done was to test all the things he believed to be true by using the method of doubt. He asked if he could possibly doubt (1) the reality of the physical world and the physical senses; (2) the validity of mathematics and the universal truths they reveal; and (3) God as supreme and good.

Doubting the reality of the physical world.　To discover if he could doubt the physical world, Descartes asked, "Is it possible for me to doubt that I am sitting in a chair in front of the fireplace, holding a newspaper in my hand?" Then, Descartes remembered that occasionally he had dreamed he was sitting in front of the fireplace with a newspaper in his hand, when actually he was lying asleep in bed. Was it possible that now, when he thought he was awake, he could actually be dreaming? Yes, he concluded, it is possible that the physical world he had thought was real could actually be a dream.

Doubting the validity of mathematics.　Yet, whether the physical world, including his own body, was real or a dream, how could he possibly doubt that two plus two always equals four?

God, being supreme and good, had created an orderly world, he argued. Therefore, mathematics is valid. Unless . . .

Doubting the goodness of God.   Descartes asked, "What if this God I thought was supremely good is actually an Evil Genius, who deceived me into thinking that mathematics is valid, and that God is good?" If God were an evil genius, then he would not be a supreme and good God, after all.

With these arguments, Descartes was able to doubt the reality of the physical world, the validity of mathematics, and even God's supreme goodness. This brought him to the conclusion there was nothing he previously believed to be true that he could not doubt.

"I Think, Therefore I Am"

Through his intuition, Descartes found one thing he could not doubt. "Though I can doubt that my body exists, or that I am awake, or that I am being deceived, I cannot doubt that I am doing the doubting." A doubter must be a thinker because you can't doubt without thinking. Thus, he concluded: "I think, therefore I am," or, "I think, therefore I exist."

For Descartes, the truth that he was a thinker was so real that he could not doubt it. He would use his thinking mind as the foundation of his philosophy. "I think, therefore I am" is Descartes's most famous and lasting legacy.

Reversal of Doubt

Descartes had not proved the reality of the physical world, the validity of mathematics, or the goodness of God. Yet he had proved intuitively that he exists as a thinker. Descartes then asked, "What is a thing that thinks?" Following his own guidelines, he deduced that a thinker "is a thing that doubts, understands, affirms, denies, wills, refuses, and that also imagines and feels."

Descartes now wanted to determine if he could reverse his doubts and prove by using his own reason as a thinker that God exists as a perfect being and not as an evil genius who deceives us into believing things as true or false.

Proving God's existence.   First, Descartes analyzed his own mind and found three types of ideas: 1) those born within him, or innate ideas; 2) ideas that he invented or imagined; and 3) ideas that came from outside him. Ideas, he said, are effects, and each effect must have a cause. In his mind, Descartes discovered that he had an "idea of perfection." He reasoned that the idea of perfection could not be innate or invented by him because he was not perfect. Based on the notion that you cannot get something more (the idea of perfection) from something less (his own imperfection), then the idea of perfection could not come from him. Therefore, the cause of the idea of perfection must have come from outside him, from a perfect being. That being is God. Descartes then defined what he meant by the name God:

> By the name God I understand a substance that is infinite, independent, all-knowing, all-powerful, and by which I myself and everything else, if anything else does exist, have been created. Now all these characteristics are such that the more diligently I attend to them, the less do they appear capable of proceeding from me alone; hence, from what has been already said, we must conclude that God necessarily exists.
>
> For although the idea of a substance is within me owing to the fact that I am substance, nevertheless I should not have the idea of an infinite substance—since I am finite—if it had not proceeded from some substance which was veritably infinite. [12]

Because God is a perfect being, Descartes argued, he could not be an evil deceiver. We know that evil is a defect, and perfection has no defects.

Proving mathematics as valid. Because mathematical statements, such as two plus two equals four, are so clear and distinct that they leave no doubt in the mind, a perfect God would not deceive me into thinking they were true if they were not. Therefore, I can accept mathematics as true.

Proving the reality of the physical world. From his own reason, Descartes proved God's perfection and the validity of mathematics. Using the same argument that God is perfect, he set out to prove that the physical world is real and not a dream: I perceive things to be present such as sight, sound, and even objects that I bump into. Such perceptions are so strong that God, being perfect, would not deceive me into believing that physical objects exist if they do not. Therefore, the physical world, including my own body, must be real and not a dream.

Mind-Body Problem

Disagreeing with Hobbes, who said that everything is matter, Descartes found that mind and matter are two separate substances, the proof being that he believed he existed as a thinker even when he doubted his physical body and the physical world. Thus, human beings are dual creatures made up of mind, or spiritual substance, and body, the physical substance. In philosophy, calling the mind one kind of substance and the body another kind of substance is known as dualism.

Descartes's conclusion left him with the problem of finding the relationship between mind and body. If mind and body are two different substances, how do they interact? He solved the problem by locating the point of connection in the pineal gland, an organ located between the two hemispheres of the brain. For

Mind	Body
Spiritual substance, or ideas	Physical substance, or matter
"I think, therefore I am"	Size, shape, motion
© Infobase Publishing	

Figure 1. Descartes's concept of dualism.

Descartes, the pineal gland joins the mind to the body, uniting them into one integral unit.

> Nature also teaches me . . . that I am not only lodged in my body as a pilot in a vessel, but that I am very closely united to it, and to speak so intermingled with it that I seem to compose with it one whole. For if that were not the case, when my body is hurt, I, who am merely a thinking thing, should not feel pain, for I should perceive this wound by the understanding only, just as the sailor perceives by sight when something is damaged in his vessel. . . .
>
> [Yet] there is a great difference between mind and body, inasmuch as body is by nature always divisible, and the mind is entirely indivisible. . . .
>
> [It follows] that the soul is really joined to the whole body [by] a certain very small gland which is situated in the middle of [the brain] and so suspended above the duct whereby the animal spirits in its anterior cavities have communication with those in the posterior, that the slightest movements which take place in it may alter very greatly the course of these spirits; and reciprocally that the smallest changes which occur in the course of the spirits may do much to change the movements of this gland. [13]

Animals as Machines

Descartes believed that all bodies are purely mechanical. The body, he said, "is like a machine." Because Descartes believed that animals do not have minds, he also believed they do not think or feel. Therefore, to Descartes, animals are merely machines. He added that, because they are machines, animals feel no pain or pleasure.

Descartes's argument gave biologists a reason to defend vivisection, the practice of operating on living animals, without anesthetic, for scientific purposes. Those who performed these surgeries coldly compared the howls and cries of a vivisected animal to the squeaks of an unoiled machine because these surgeons did not connect the animal's agonizing cries with pain.

Benedict de Spinoza

In response to Descartes's dualism, the Dutch Jewish philosopher Benedict de Spinoza discovered a new way of viewing the mind-body problem and God. Considered one of the greatest Continental rationalists, Benedict de Spinoza's scientific and philosophical accomplishments helped lay the foundation for modern biblical criticism. Comparisons of Spinoza to the great Greek philosopher Socrates have been made for centuries.

> Except for Socrates himself it would be hard to find a philosopher who was a more highly regarded person than Benedict (Baruch) Spinoza. Like Socrates, he was not interested in power or wealth. Like Socrates, he was accused of atheism and was hounded for his unorthodox beliefs. And, like Socrates, he was interested in philosophy as a way of life, not as a professional discipline. [14]

Spinoza's Life

Benedict (Baruch) de Spinoza (1632–1677) was born in Amsterdam, the Netherlands, the son of a wealthy Jewish merchant who had fled religious persecution in Portugal. His parents educated him in the traditional Hebrew literature, hoping he

Benedict de Spinoza's contention that God is the world and the world is in God summarized his belief that there is no separation between God and the world. Spinoza was excommunicated by the Jewish community for his beliefs.

would become a rabbi. Because of his original ideas on God and nature, however, the Jewish community accused him of heresy. The synagogue of Amsterdam insisted that Spinoza renounce his personal philosophy. When he refused, they officially excommunicated him with a curse:

> With the judgment of the angels and the sentence of the saints, we anathematize, execrate, curse and cast out Baruch Spinoza. . . . Let him be accursed by day, and accursed by night; let him be accursed in his lying down, and accursed in his rising up; accursed in going out and accursed in coming in. May the Lord never more pardon or acknowledge him; may the wrath and displeasure of the Lord burn henceforth against this man, load him with all the curses written in the Book of the Law, and blot out his name from under the sky.[15]

Even Spinoza's own family disowned him. When someone tried to kill him, he changed his name from Baruch to Benedict and left Amsterdam for the Hague, another large Netherlands city. There, he lived a secluded life devoted to philosophy, earning a meager living by grinding lenses. His kindness and simplicity was an example to others as was his reputation as a brilliant philosopher. Spinoza was offered a professorship of philosophy by the University of Heidelberg in Germany, but he refused the offer so that he could maintain the freedom he needed to write his own philosophy. Spinoza died at age 44 of tuberculosis, probably as a result of breathing the glass dust from the lenses he ground.

God

Like Descartes, Spinoza wanted to develop what he called a "geometry of philosophy" to explain the nature of reality. In his masterwork, *Ethics*, Spinoza said if we are to understand the

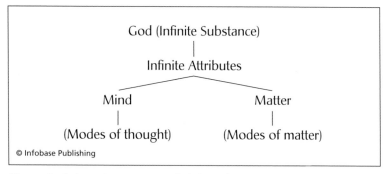

Figure 2. Spinoza's geometry of philosophy.

universe and human nature, we must first formulate ideas about God. He agreed with Descartes that God is an "infinite substance," but he disagreed that mind and matter are two separate substances. God did not create the world to stand outside it, he insisted. God is the world, and the world is in God. There is no separation between God and the world. Thus, Spinoza rejected Descartes's dualistic view that God is separate from the world. For Spinoza, God is "one substance with infinite attributes," or expressions, meaning that mind and matter are two attributes of God's one substance and not two different substances. Being infinite, God contains everything.

Spinoza's statement that God contains everything makes Spinoza a pantheist, a view unacceptable to Jewish and Christian theologians. According to Judaism and Christianity, God created nature and finite beings, and his creations are separate and dependent on him. Spinoza had no quarrel that God is ultimate reality, but he denied that God is a person, a creator, or a loving father. For Spinoza, God, as "infinite substance," goes beyond these human qualities, yet contains everything.

The World

As a pantheist, Spinoza viewed the world as modes, or shapes and appearances, of God's existence. This idea also opposed

Jewish and Christian belief that the world is separate from God. According to Spinoza, the world is God expressed in various modes of mind and matter. Modes differ from attributes only in degree, not in kind. Your body, for example, is a mode of matter, and your mind is a mode of thought. A rose is a mode of the attribute of matter, and a poem about the rose is a mode of the attribute of thought. Both, however, are expressions of God.

Freedom

Because everything, including our thoughts and actions, is an expression of God and follows God's laws, we can only act according to our nature. For Spinoza, the belief that we are free comes from our ignorance of the causes and desires that motivate us. For instance, when we judge people to be good or bad, we are essentially saying they could have acted differently. Spinoza argued, however, that good and bad are relative to human standards, not to those of God. Only when we realize that the cause of what happens to us comes from the nature of God will we understand.

Free will is only in God. The free individual, led by reason and intuition, wills to understand God's law. Thus, the highest human happiness springs from our knowledge of God. The more we understand God, the freer we are.

> It is therefore most profitable to us in life to make perfect the intellect or reason as far as possible, and in this one thing consists the highest happiness or blessedness of man; for blessedness is nothing but the peace of mind which springs from the intuitive knowledge of God, and to perfect the intellect is nothing but to understand God, together with the attributes and actions of God, which flow from the necessity of His nature.[16]

If the way . . . I have shown . . . seems very difficult, it can nevertheless be found. It must indeed be difficult since it is so seldom discovered; for if salvation lay ready to hand and could be discovered without great labour, how could it be possible that it should be neglected almost by everybody? But all noble things are as difficult as they are rare. [17]

Gottfried Wilhelm von Leibniz

Although Gottfried Liebniz was impressed with Spinoza's philosophy, he disagreed with his idea of God as one infinite substance. One of Leibniz's projects was an attempt to reconcile Protestants and Catholics and bring about a union between Christian states.

Liebniz's Life

Baron Gottfried Wilhelm von Leibniz (1646–1716) was born in Leipzig, a city in the German state of Saxony. A child genius, at age 13, he was reading advanced scholastic treatises, and at age 15, he entered the University of Leipzig to study philosophy. Two years later, he enrolled in the University of Jena to study mathematics and law. The following year, he published a treatise on law, and at 21, he received a doctorate of law degree. He then entered the civil service, in which he had a distinguished career.

Independently of Isaac Newton, Leibniz invented calculus, although each accused the other of stealing his ideas. Leibniz was also a diplomat, an administrator, and a historian for the duke of Hanover. In his spare time, he traveled widely and corresponded with hundreds of people. During this period, he tried to bridge the disagreements that divided Catholics and Protestants. He also authored numerous works that later influenced major philosophers such as Immanuel Kant and Bertrand Russell. Despite his accomplishments, Leibniz's public influence took a nosedive into oblivion, and when he died, his secretary was his only mourner.

Monads

Leibniz rejected both Descartes's and Spinoza's ideas of substance. According to Leibniz, when Descartes distinguished mind and body as two different substances, he ran into the problem of trying to explain how the mind and the body interact. Spinoza had tried to solve the problem by saying there is one substance with attributes of both mind and body. Leibniz did not accept either answer.

Leibniz developed a new theory about substances he called "monads," from the Greek *monos*, meaning "one." If you looked at matter, he said, then you would find it is made up of indivisible things that have no parts. Monads are these undividable things. A monad is an indivisible point that is independent of other monads. Each monad has within itself an internal principle that causes it to change. There is no outside cause-and-effect influence between monads. For Leibniz, however, there is a "preestablished harmony" that God created for each monad to "mirror" others.

> There is . . . no way of explaining how a monad can be altered or changed in its inner being by any other creature, for . . . the monads have no windows through which anything can enter or depart . . . .
>
> The natural changes of the monads proceed from an internal principle, since an external cause could not influence their inner being. [18]

God's Clock

Because monads have no "windows," they are not open to influence by other monads but open only to God who brings the monads into perfect harmony. God creates each monad to carry out its preestablished harmony, which means the universe is an orderly, harmonious system. Leibniz said the universe is "God's clock," and it keeps perfect time. He compared the monads to "several different bands of musicians and choirs playing their own notes" in perfect harmony.

The monads mirror the world in different ways and with different levels of awareness. Rocks are on a lower level of awareness than are humans. The human soul monad is higher than the human body monad. According to Leibniz, the highest monad in a person is a spirit monad that could know the universe and relate with the highest monad of all—God.

The Problem of Evil

What puzzled Leibniz about a harmonious universe is the possibility of evil. He believed that God is perfect and good, and that God created the "best of all possible worlds." Yet, within the world, we find disorder and evil. As Leibniz probed deeply into this subject, he found, like Augustine, that anything less than God has to be limited, and depending on the extent of its limitation, we find imperfection or evil. Thus, evil is found in the very nature of any world that God might choose to create. Yet, as imperfect as our world is, it is the best possible world God could have created.

God could produce a world with the greatest amount of good only by creating one in which evil would exist. To illustrate his belief, Leibniz used the analogy of how the downstream motion of a river carries boats along with it, and the heavier the boats are, the slower they move. God is the cause of perfection in the nature of creatures, but the limitation of the creature's ability to receive perfection is the cause of imperfection, which is evil. Evil, then, is the absence of perfection.

God preestablishes harmony in each monad and gives it a purpose. We are free when we cut through confused thoughts and follow the purpose that God has given us.

LINKS TO BRITISH EMPIRICISM

Bold ventures of the mind filled the first centuries of modern philosophical thought. It was a time of freedom for philosophers to formulate systems of truth based on clear, rational principles. Rationalism, a new intellectual mood of modern philosophy, stressed scientific observation and mathematics. Rationalists accepted, almost without question, the intellectual powers of the rational mind.

Yet, some philosophers felt uneasy about the sweeping speculations of the rationalists, and philosophy began to take a new turn. These philosophers, known as the British empiricists, questioned the ability of the mind to know God, the universe, or human nature. Like the Skeptics of ancient Greece, the empiricists asked if knowledge, as something certain, is even possible at all.

3

THE BRITISH EMPIRICISTS
Locke, Berkeley, and Hume

*Reason is, and ought only to be the slave
of the passions, and can never pretend to
any other office than to serve and obey them.*
—David Hume

THE EMPIRICISTS

Since Plato, rationalists have thought that true knowledge is innate in the reason, and if we use reason properly, we could know the meaning of human existence and the universe. The leading rationalists in the seventeenth century were Descartes, who was French; Spinoza, who was Dutch; and Leibniz, who was German. The three leading empiricists in modern philosophy are all British: John Locke from England, George Berkeley from Ireland, and David Hume from Scotland. All three British empiricists disagreed with the rationalists. They believed that the mind has no innate knowledge, and that the only way to understand the world is through our sense experience.

John Locke, the founder of the school of empiricism, said that human knowledge is limited to our own experience. The word empiricism comes from the Greek root *emperiria*, which means "experience." Locke questioned the notion of innate ideas. He did not think we could ever understand the true nature of

Rationalists	Empiricists
Knowledge comes from the reason.	Knowledge comes from sense experience.
Knowledge is *a priori*, or innate.	Knowledge is *a posteriori*, or based on experience.
Knowledge is universally true.	We can never know anything that is beyond the realm of immediate experience.
© Infobase Publishing	

Figure 3. A comparison between the Continental rationalism of Descartes, Spinoza, and Leibniz and the philosophies of British empiricists Locke, Berkeley, and Hume.

the universe. George Berkeley went even further by questioning the existence of matter. David Hume asked whether any knowledge is possible at all!

John Locke

Locke is famous for saying the mind is a *tabula rasa*, or an empty slate. He said there is nothing in the mind except what comes from the senses. When, for instance, we use words like God, eternity, or the philosophical "substance," we do not really know what we are talking about because nobody has experienced God, eternity, or substance. Yet, although we cannot know God, said Locke, when we reflect on our experiences, we can conclude that God exists.

Locke's Life

John Locke (1632–1704) grew up in a Puritan home in which his parents believed in the virtues of hard work. His father, a lawyer and small landowner, fought on the side of the Parliament against Charles I during the English Civil War (1642–1651), and like his father, John Locke was a lifetime defender of the parliamentary system. As a teenager, Locke attended Westminster School in London and then received a scholarship at Oxford University, where he took the bachelor's and master's degrees. His interest in science led him to study medicine, yet he was also interested in political questions such as the relation of church and state and the importance of religious toleration. He decided to put medical school on hold while he went on a diplomatic mission. When he returned to England, he entered the political world and developed a friendship with Lord Ashley, who later became the earl of Shaftesbury. While involved with political life, Locke managed to finish his medical degree. Soon after, he saved Lord Ashley's life by operating on an "internal abscess."

When Lord Ashley led Parliament against King James II, the king strongly suspected Locke's influence on the plot to remove him, although there is little evidence of Locke's involvement. Fearing retribution from the king, Locke fled to Holland in 1683 as an advisor to Prince William and Princess Mary of Orange. After the revolution that overthrew King James II in 1688, Locke returned home with William and Mary, the new king and queen of England. At last, Locke was free to fight for his favorite ideas—freedom of the press, religious toleration, new educational programs, help for the poor, and economic changes.

In his influential essay on civil government, "Second Treatise of Government," Locke proposed ideas that may sound familiar to most Americans: that all men are "equal and independent" and possess the natural rights to "life, health, liberty, and possessions." Such essays by Locke helped America's founders shape the Declaration of Independence and the United States Constitution.

A religious man, Locke spent his retirement years studying scripture, especially the Epistles of St. Paul. At age 72, he died at a friend's home.

The Human Mind

One night, while Locke and some friends were discussing philosophy, they spoke about how the human mind works. They knew that the Continental rationalists considered mathematical reasoning as the ultimate knowledge. Locke, however, took a more practical approach. He told his associates about the "internal abscess" of his friend Lord Ashley. If Locke had waited for "mathematical certainty about the treatment," then the patient would have died. So, he decided to operate. During the surgery, Locke took careful notes of his surgical procedure for other doctors to use if the operation was a success. The patient lived.

Locke decided that knowledge results not from reason alone but from ideas based on experience. Such experience, he said, takes two forms: sensation and reflection. First, we experience objects with our senses, and then we reflect on them with our reason. Plato, Descartes, and the other rationalists had thought that we are born with innate ideas. Locke, however, said at birth our mind is a tabula rasa, and on this "blank white paper" our experiences are written.

Because the mind is blank at birth, the senses must relay to it such qualities as yellowness, heat, softness, hardness, sweetness, and bitterness. When we reflect on these qualities, the mind receives ideas such as thinking, doubting, believing, knowing, and willing. Yet, these ideas occur only after our mind has had a sense experience.

> All ideas come from sensation or reflection— Let us suppose the mind to be, as we say, white paper, void of all characters, without any ideas: —How comes it to be furnished? . . . Whence has it all the materials of reason and knowledge? To this I answer, in one word, from EXPERIENCE. In that all our knowledge is founded; and from that it ultimately derives itself. Our observation employed

John Locke's concept of tabula rasa stated that the human mind at birth is "blank," upon which our sensory experiences add information and ways of processing information. Locke believed that individuals have the freedom to define their own characters.

either about external sensible objects, or about the internal operations of our minds perceived and reflected on by ourselves, is that which supplies our understandings with all the materials of thinking. These two are the fountains of knowledge, from whence all the ideas we have, or can naturally have, do spring. [19]

Knowledge

Locke raised the question regarding how much knowledge we could have. He decided that knowledge depends on how our ideas relate to each other. The way ideas relate to each other depends on our perceptions. Locke discovered three kinds of perception: (1) intuitive, (2) demonstrative, and (3) sensitive.

Intuitive knowledge is direct knowing that leaves no doubt in our mind. "It is the clearest and most certain" knowledge we humans have. We know intuitively that we exist, that a straight line is not a curve, and that the number three is not the number five.

Demonstrative knowledge starts with an intuition and then leads the mind step-by-step to know the agreement and disagreement between one idea and another. The idea of God, said Locke, starts with an intuition of our own existence; then, by demonstration, reason leads us to the knowledge that something must have produced our existence, "that there is an eternal, most powerful, and most knowing Being."

Sensitive knowledge, according to Locke, only "passes under the name of knowledge." We see a flower. We know the flower exists. Yet, when we walk away, we are no longer sure the flower exists. Because our senses do not tell us how things are connected, they can give us some knowledge, but never certainty.

Because we are not fit to deal with metaphysical questions regarding God, truth, and substance, questions which had been the focus of many earlier philosophers, Locke thought metaphysics was useless and even harmful because it distracts us from more important matters such as politics and morality.

Moral Philosophy

For Locke, there are no innate ideas. Therefore, moral, religious, and political values must come from our experience. The word *good*, for example, refers to pleasure, and the word *evil* implies pain. We cannot define words such as pleasure and pain, but we can know them by experience. Morality, then, has to do with choosing and willing the good. Unlike Socrates and Plato, who claimed that if we know the good then we will do the good, Locke said we do not always act on what we know. The smoker knows that cigarettes cause lung cancer, yet he continues to smoke. The smoker sees the greater good but chooses a lesser good to avoid the immediate pain of not having a cigarette.

> Let a drunkard see that his health decays, his estate wastes; discredit and diseases, and the want of all things, even of his beloved drink, attends him in the course he follows; yet the . . . habitual thirst after his cups . . . drives him to the tavern. . . . It is not want of viewing the greater good: for he sees and acknowledges it. [20]

For Locke, then, moral good is the conformity and moral evil is the nonconformity of our actions to one of three laws: (1) law of opinion; (2) civil law; and (3) divine law. The law of opinion constitutes the laws of our society. In our society, we tend to call actions that we judge to be admirable as good actions, and those that we judge to be irresponsible as bad ones. If you conform to public opinion, then you are good. Remember, however, that different societies have different ideas of what is good. Civil law is set up by the society and enforced by the courts and the police. The law of opinion and civil law usually overlap.

According to Locke, divine law is God's law, the only true law for our behavior. The law of opinion and the civil law should always conform to the divine law.

> He [God] has a right to do it; we are his creatures . . . and he has power to enforce it by rewards and punishments . . . in another life. . . . This is the only true touchstone of moral rectitude; and, by comparing them to this law it is that men judge of the most considerable moral good or evil of their actions. [21]

The difference among these three laws lies in our choosing immediate pleasures over future pleasures. For Locke, the divine law is eternally true and the one we should follow.

Political Philosophy

For Hobbes, "the state of nature" was our need to survive. For Locke, the state of nature is a moral state given to us by God that includes the right to life, health, liberty, and private property.

Locke and Hobbes agreed that there should be a social contract between the people and their government, but they disagreed on what the social contract meant. Hobbes thought the people should be servants of the authority in power. Locke took the opposite stance. His social contract allowed the people to delegate power to the legislature. Thus, when people hand over power to the government, the government becomes the servant of the people.

Bishop George Berkeley

Whereas Locke, Descartes, Spinoza, and Leibniz believed that the physical world is real, Berkeley questioned that we actually perceive matter. He believed we do not perceive matter as solid because perception itself is not physical. Perception and everything else is God's spirit. Berkeley is noted for saying, "To be is to be perceived."

Berkeley's Life

George Berkeley (pronounced Bark-lee) (1685–1753) was born in Ireland. At age 15, he entered Trinity College in Dublin to study philosophy. While there, he became a fellow of the college and an ordained Anglican priest.

For 11 years after graduation, he traveled widely and met many of the thinkers of the day, including Joseph Addison and

Jonathan Swift. During his stay in London, he asked Parliament to finance his project of founding a college in Bermuda to teach the Gospel and English manners to the "American savages." With the promise of financial support, he and his wife sailed for

George Berkeley believed everything that exists has a mind, or depends for its existence on a mind. Berkeley took the bold position that physical objects, or matter, do not exist. Berkeley's belief regarding the nature of objects is called "immaterialism."

America. After arriving in Rhode Island, he waited three years for the money but it never arrived. Finally, he gave up and returned to Ireland to become the bishop of Cloyne.

Berkeley opposed scientific materialism because he saw science as dangerous to the Christian way of life and as a threat to faith in God. God, he said, created nature and preserves nature. Science interferes with God's creation. Berkeley proposed education as a cure to poverty and promoted the medicinal value of "tar-water," which he made from pine tree pitch, a remedy he learned from the American Indians. In fact, he often prescribed tar-water to members of his diocese as a cure for illness as well as aches and pains.

When his oldest son died, Berkeley and his family moved to Oxford, where another son attended college. A year later, at age 68, Berkeley died unexpectedly. In his will, he asked that his body not be buried "until it grows offensive by the cadaverous smell." We do not know whether his family waited that long.

One of the United States' leading university towns, Berkeley, California, is named for him. His Rhode Island home, White Hall, was designated a United States First National Monument and still stands today.

To Be Is to Be Perceived

As an empiricist, Berkeley agreed with Locke that we could only know what we perceive through the senses. Yet, Berkeley went a step further when he added that we do not perceive matter. We do not see physical objects as solid because our perception itself is not a material thing.

We do, he said, experience sensations or ideas such as color, taste, smell, size, and shape. Yet, objects that do not have color, taste, smell, size, and shape cannot exist because we find no matter in them. Physical objects, then, are clusters of ideas or sensations, and only exist when a mind perceives them.

His thinking produced the shocking conclusion, "To be is to be perceived." This conclusion means that, when we do not perceive an object, we have no idea if it exists or not.

Through the eyes of Berkeley's philosophy, when a person looks at a dog on a sofa, he or she experiences the sensation of seeing a dog on the sofa. The dog that appears in the person's perception is an idea and not physical matter. The dog and the sofa consist of the same ingredients as his or her sensation. All physical things such as computers, books, apples, horses, and people exist only if there is some mind to perceive them.

Berkeley did not deny that the physical world exists. If it did not exist, we could not experience it. He said this, however: Matter that makes up the physical world is not a true substance. The only true substance is the substance of God and the human mind, which is a thinking substance. No unthinking substance exists. This line of reasoning puts Berkeley in the philosophical school called idealism, in which spirit is reality.

Yet, if "to be is to be perceived," what happens to the dog and the sofa when the person leaves the room? What happens to any object when there is no one around to perceive it?

Over a century after Berkeley put forth this question, Ronald Knox, an English theologian and writer, created the following two-part limerick and posted it on a tree in a college quad:

There was a young man who said, "God
Must think it exceedingly odd
If he finds that this tree
Continues to be
When there's no one about in the Quad."
(the reply):
Dear Sir: Your astonishment's odd:
I am always about in the Quad.
And that's why this tree

Will continue to be,
Since observed by
Yours faithfully,
God.

"God's" reply in the limerick was how Berkeley would answer the first part of the limerick; namely, that objects external to our minds exist when we do not see them. There exists, Berkeley said, an "omnipresent eternal mind" that knows everything and reveals it to our view. Everything we see and feel is "an effect of God's power." The whole world and our whole life exist only in the mind of God.

David Hume

David Hume, the last of these great British empiricists, considered the philosophies of Locke and Berkeley so valuable that he followed them to their logical conclusion. He is also significant as the person who set the famous philosopher Immanuel Kant on the road to his philosophy. Hume asked the question, "Can we even know if the physical world exists?"

Hume's Life

David Hume (1711–1776) was born in Edinburgh, Scotland, the son of a lawyer. When he was two years old, his father died, and his deeply religious mother raised him. For a brief period during his childhood, Hume was very pious, worrying about his vices, especially about his pride. At the age of 12, he enrolled in the University of Edinburgh, and shortly after, he lost his faith. His mother hoped he would follow his father into law, but Hume found law distasteful compared to philosophy. After three years, he left the university to devote himself to philosophy, and after reading Locke and other philosophers, he lost all belief in religion.

Hume moved to La Flèche, France, where he wrote his first philosophical work, *A Treatise of Human Nature*. He hoped this work would bring him fame and fortune, but it "fell still-born from the press." In other words, no one read it.

For the next 13 years, Hume tutored to an insane marquis and was secretary to a general. He continued to write philosophy and became highly successful. Hume accepted the position of librarian for the Faculty of Advocates in Edinburgh, and wrote a six-volume set entitled *History of England*. His unconventional ideas, however, led to controversy, and the curators asked him to resign.

When he returned to France as secretary to the British ambassador, the French intellectual society treated him as a celebrity. They admired his writings and sought his company. In 1765, when he returned to Edinburgh, his house became the hub for intellectual gatherings. In the spring of 1775, Hume developed cancer, and he died the next year.

How the Mind Works

By following the empirical methods of Locke and Berkeley, Hume hoped to clear up what he called the "fuzzy thinking" of past philosophers. He wanted to do for human nature what Isaac Newton did for physical nature: to give an explanation of how the mind works. At first, Hume was optimistic, but as he traced the process of how we form ideas and discovered the limitations of the human mind, his optimism soon turned to skepticism.

Nothing, at first view, may seem more unbounded than the thought of man, which not only escapes all human power and authority, but is not even restrained within the limits of nature and reality. To form monsters, and join incongruous shapes and appearances, costs the imagination no more trouble than to conceive the most natural and familiar objects. And while the body is confined to one planet . . . the thought can in an instant transport us into the most distant regions of the universe. . . . But though our thought seems to possess this unbounded liberty, we shall find, upon a nearer examination, that it is really confined within very narrow limits, and that all this creative power of the mind amounts to no more than the faculty of compounding, transposing, augmenting, or diminishing the materials afforded us by the senses and experience. [22]

At first, Hume thought that, although our physical bodies are confined to the planet, our minds could go anyplace in the universe. After a closer look, however, he found that our thoughts are really confined to our sense experience, which he called "perceptions." We have, said Hume, two types of perceptions: impressions and ideas. By impressions, he meant our sense experience of the external world. By ideas, he meant our memory of these impressions. Impressions and ideas make up the total contents of the mind.

Impressions are much more vivid than the ideas that these impressions produce. For instance, if you burn your hand on a hot stove, you get an immediate impression. Many months later, you may remember the burning incident, but your memory is less vivid than the original painful impression.

Without impressions, Hume said, we have no ideas, because "ideas are copies of impressions." For every idea we must first have an impression.

For Hume, there are simple ideas and complex ideas. A simple idea is a single idea: I saw a bird. A complex idea consists of more than one idea, such as imagining a flying red horse. Through our senses we have perceived impressions, such as wings, horses, and the color red. A flying red horse, however, is a false idea that we must reject if we want to tidy up our thoughts. Hume gave the example of a golden mountain to illustrate his point:

> When we think of a golden mountain, we only join two consistent ideas, *gold* and *mountain*, with which we were formerly acquainted. A virtuous horse we can conceive; because, from our own feeling, we can conceive virtue; and this we may unite to the figure and shape of a horse, which is an animal familiar to us. In short, all the materials of thinking are derived either from our outward or inward sentiment: the mixture and composition of these belongs alone to the mind and will. Or, to express myself in philosophical language, all our ideas or more feeble perceptions are copies of our impressions or more lively ones. [23]

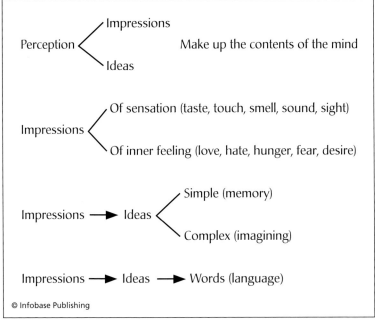

Figure 4. A diagram of Hume's contents of the mind. In the bottom schematic, words are meaningful only if they can be traced to impressions or to ideas that copy impressions.

Relations of Ideas

Hume believed we know the relations of ideas by using our reason instead of sense impressions. Yet, these relations of ideas give us no information about what exists because we need sense impressions to know what exists. For example, two plus two equals four expresses a relation between numbers. Although true, such truths are empty because they give us no information about matters of fact or the world of our experience.

Matters of fact, such as the Sun will rise tomorrow, are not certain. They may or may not happen. We cannot demonstrate the truth or falsehood of the statement, "The sun will rise tomorrow." We may think we know things beyond our senses, but we cannot prove it. How do we know that the future will be like the past? With this unusual finding, Hume looked at the idea of cause and effect with new skepticism.

Cause and Effect

Hume stubbornly asked, "Is there an impression that gives us the idea of cause and effect?" "Is there a necessary connection between a cause and an effect?" He found none. So how do we get the idea of cause and effect?

Hume decided the idea must arise when we experience certain relations between objects. When we speak of cause and effect, we are saying that A causes B. For instance, you are watching billiard players. You see the cue ball (A) hit and (B) move the eight ball. Obviously, A caused B. Wait, said Hume. If you pay close attention, you will realize that you did not see the cue ball move the eight ball. You saw a sequence of events: (1) contiguity (A and B are always close together); (2) priority in time (A always precedes B); and (3) constant conjunction (B always follows A). From these events, you conclude that a "necessary connection" exists, but contiguity, priority, and constant conjunction do not imply a necessary connection between objects. Therefore, Hume said, "Necessity is something in the mind, and not in the objects." Neither cause nor effect is in the objects we observe, but only our "habit of association." For that reason, cause and effect cannot be the basis for scientific or any other kind of knowledge.

The External World

Hume has taken us along a bumpy road. He questioned everything we thought to be true. He even asked, "Does the physical, or external, world exist?" He did not say that the external world does not exist but only that we cannot know if it exists. "Let us chase our imagination to the heavens, or to the utmost limits of the universe," challenged Hume, believing we can never get a step beyond ourselves. In other words, we are prisoners of our own sense experiences. There is no way to get outside them because all we can know is what we experience—our own private sensations and impressions. Your friend may agree with you that the apple you are sharing is sour. Yet, how do you know what your friend is really experiencing? Can you know if it is the same experience you are having?

The Self (Soul)

Throughout history, philosophers have struggled with the question of human nature and our relationship to the world. Plato thought that our true nature is in the soul, which is distinct from the body. The soul exists before the body is born, stays with the body temporarily, and survives the death of the body. For the atomists, another school of early Greek philosophic thought, the soul is made of atoms, which is matter. Aristotle viewed the soul as born with the body but not surviving in a personal way after death. The medieval philosophers believed God created the soul with the possibility of individual salvation.

In the modern era, Descartes considered the soul or mind a spiritual substance, and immortal. By contrast, Hobbes saw humans only as matter and therefore not immortal. From the beginning of philosophy, there had been no consensus on the subject of soul or mind in human nature. Hume wanted to know if he could have an impression of a soul, which he called "the self."

The self, said Hume, supposedly accounts for the idea that I am the same person today as I was as a baby. Most of my characteristics have changed over the years: I no longer cry for food,

Scottish philosopher David Hume questioned that we could know for certain the laws of nature, claiming, however, that they are probable. To Hume, cause and effect were habits of our association and should not provide the basis for scientific knowledge.

wear diapers, or have the emotions of a baby, yet I am the same person. Is this "I" a permanent self? asked Hume. He came to the conclusion that we have *no* idea of a self. All we have are "bundles of perceptions" of things like heat or cold, light or shade, love or hate, and pain or pleasure. Hume decided that the idea of a self is like the idea of cause and effect. We think the self and cause and effect are facts, but they are fictions. According to Hume, believing in a permanent, unchanging self or soul is merely an act "of the imagination." He concluded that we have no "personal identity," no permanent "I," but only perceptions and feelings that come and go.

> For my part, when I enter most intimately into what I call *myself*, I always stumble on some particular perception or other, of heat or cold, light or shade, love or hatred, pain or pleasure. I never can catch *myself* at any time without a perception, and never can observe any thing but the perception. . . . The mind is a kind of theatre, where several perceptions successively make their appearance; pass, re-pass, glide away, and mingle in an infinite variety of postures and situations. There is properly no *simplicity* in it at one time, nor *identity* in different. . . . The comparison of the theatre must not mislead us. They are the successive perceptions only that constitute the mind. [24]

Next, Hume put God to the same test that he put the self.

God

Hume could not accept Descartes's idea of God as an idea that comes from outside our mind because for Hume "our ideas reach no further than our experience." As he looked at the world around him, Hume thought he might argue for God as a designer of an orderly universe. Each year there is fall, winter, spring, and summer. We sense "the divine" in a beautiful sunrise, a noble horse, and a wild flower. We attribute these beauties to an intelligent designer, God. Yet Hume saw how destructive living things in the world were to each other. "The world is contemptible," he said. "Nature is blind and without discernment." Because we have no impression in nature of an orderly designer, he decided we could have no idea of a God. Therefore, the word God is a meaningless term.

Moral Philosophy

Most philosophers before the British empiricists thought that we should rely on reason for moral judgments. Hume disagreed. Reason plays a role in moral decisions, but moral judgments, he said, are mainly sentiment (sympathy or feeling), especially what he called "fellow feelings," or the ability to experience another person's good or pain as if it were our own.

Hume asked us to consider an act of murder. Can you find anything in the facts of any murder case that reveals the act is morally wrong? The facts merely show that one person ended the life of another in a certain way at a certain time and place. Our reason tells us how long it took for death to occur, the weapon used, where the crime took place, and other facts. But reason cannot show us the moral wrongfulness of the act. The notion of wrong arises in our sentiment toward the action. When we call an act immoral, we are using our feeling judgment only, not the reason.

Hume concluded that sentiment is the basis for all value judgments as well as for moral judgments. Even the kind of music you like is not a rational choice but the sentiment of sympathy. With reason you can tell the arrangement of the notes and which instruments are playing the piece, but reason cannot decide if you like or dislike the music.

Human beings are morally sensitive creatures. What we consider good pleases us. Actions that offend us, we consider bad. Moral judgments come from our goodwill. We do not like to see others suffer. Because sentiments differ among societies, it is the job of reason to judge which practice is the best for each society.

LINKS TO IMMANUEL KANT

The most important discovery of the British empiricists was Hume's discovery that there is no "necessary connection" between cause and effect. This view stunned scientists and philosophers. Other empiricists' views were also revolutionary, but Hume took them to their logical conclusion: Reason tells us nothing about the world we live in. Such skepticism drove a wedge between reason and nature, and it was this wedge that woke Immanuel Kant from his "dogmatic slumbers." Struck by the destructive potential of Hume's findings to philosophy and science, Kant wanted to answer Hume by analyzing the capacity of the mind. His conclusions represent one of the important turning points in Western philosophy.

4

CRITICAL PHILOSOPHY
Immanuel Kant

*Two things fill the mind with ever new
and increasing admiration and awe . . .
the starry heavens above
and the moral law within.*
—Immanuel Kant

CRITICAL PHILOSOPHY

Until he read the British empiricists, Kant was satisfied with the direction philosophy was taking. But when he read David Hume, Kant was awakened, claiming that Hume "woke me from my dogmatic slumbers." The empiricists had argued that the mind conforms to the world it perceives: first from sense impressions, then from ideas that come from these impressions. The mind conforms to the world, which means the mind is passive. Not true, said Kant. The mind takes an active part in knowing the world. *The mind does not conform to the world—the world conforms to the mind.* Kant also did not agree with the Continental rationalists who argued that by reason alone we could know God, freedom, and immortality.

Wanting to avoid the extreme positions of the empiricists and the rationalists, Kant went to work to put "philosophy back in the saddle." His greatness was his ability to mend the split between rationalism and empiricism. Because he critiqued the powers of the mind, Kant's philosophy is known as Critical philosophy. Like Plato and Aristotle, Kant's philosophy is one of the most important turning points in Western thought.

Kant's Life

Immanuel Kant (1724–1804) was born in Königsberg in East Prussia (present-day Kaliningrad in western Russia) to strict Lutheran parents. His father made leather straps and used them regularly on his 11 children. His mother was a stern Puritan who insisted on rigorous moral standards. When Kant became an adult, he broke away from the church but remained a deeply spiritual man.

At 16, Kant enrolled in the University of Königsberg to study philosophy and physics. Other than a tutoring job in a neighboring village, Kant never traveled more than 15 miles from his home. He studied the Oriental philosophers, who had a strong influence on him, but he had yet to develop a philosophy of his own. Of himself, he said, "I have the fortune to be a lover of philosophy, but my mistress [philosophy] has shown me few favors as yet."

For 15 years, Kant taught at the University of Königsberg. He preferred students who had only average academic abilities. Kant said, "The geniuses are in no need of my help, and the dunces are beyond all help." Students described him as a professor who used words six feet long to express unimportant thoughts. One of his students remarked, "He carries us over a sea without shores in a vessel without sails." Nevertheless, his classes were popular and well attended.

Kant led a strangely uneventful life. He never married, never was sick, and his biographies relate that he was so precise in his daily habits that his neighbors could set their clocks by his routine. Each afternoon at exactly three thirty, he left his house for a walk. Only once did he fail to appear. That day, the towns-people thought he was ill and went to his house to see what was wrong. When they arrived, they found Kant—totally absorbed, calmly reading French philosopher Jean-Jacques Rousseau's *Emile*, a book that profoundly affected Kant's philosophy.

Kant was approximately five feet tall, with a flat chest, a protruding stomach, humped shoulders, and head perched to one side. He wore a gray hat, a gray coat, gray trousers, and carried a gray cane. Walking behind him, holding an umbrella in the event of rain, was his faithful servant, Lampe. Kant was a popular host, and friends loved to converse with him. No one really knew that a volcano of ideas was percolating in his mod-est head. Kant was 57 when he was awakened by Hume's work. Kant's ideas then erupted into the most remarkable philosoph-ical system of modern times, earning him the title of the father of German Idealism. Kant's success in negotiating the dead-lock between rationalism and empiricism ended an era in the history of philosophy. When Kant died at age 80, these words were inscribed on his tombstone:

> *Two Things Fill My Mind With Ever-Increasing Wonder and Awe,*
> *The Starry Heavens Above Me*
> *And the Moral Law Within Me*

Kant's Revolution

Kant thought that the rational views of Descartes, Spinoza, and Leibniz, and the empirical views of Locke, Berkeley, and Hume were partly right and partly wrong. The empiricists believed that the world impresses things on our minds. Locke had said the mind at birth is a blank tablet on which the senses write. Hume had said all our knowledge relies on sense impressions

Immanuel Kant argued that we could never really know if there was God and an afterlife because of the limitations of our reason. He added, however, that we could never really know that there *was not* God and an afterlife. For the general good of society, Kant said people were justified in believing in them.

and we can only know our own experiences and ideas. We cannot have knowledge of cause and effect because we associate two events merely from habit. We have no true knowledge of the physical world because we are stuck with our own personal experiences and ideas.

Kant agreed with Hume and the empiricists that our knowledge *begins* with sense experience, but, he insisted, it does not *end* with sense experience. He agreed with the rationalists that our reason has certain innate abilities that determine how we see the world. In other words, our mind is not simply passive; it *acts*, and reason gives us information about the world. Kant also thought that the rationalists went too far in their claims about how much reason could know.

Kant compared his philosophy to the Copernican revolution in astronomy. Before Copernicus, scholars believed Earth was the center of the universe and that all heavenly bodies revolved around it. Copernicus, however, proved that the Sun is the center of our solar system and Earth and other planets orbit it. Kant's "revolution" was the claim that the world conforms to the mind. The mind does not conform to the world, as Hume had said. Our knowledge begins with experience, but the reason does not totally rely on the senses for information, because the reason has powers of its own: the ability to organize the objects we see. For Kant, however, the rationalists also were mistaken in thinking that we could know God, freedom, or immortality, because the mind cannot comprehend such things. If it could, all rational people would have the same definition of God, freedom, and immortality.

Two Types of Knowledge

Kant said we have two types of knowledge: (1) *a priori*, or innate; and (2) *a posteriori*, or knowledge based on sense experience.

A priori ideas are innate ideas that the reason can know without using the senses. That is why we can have knowledge of cause and effect. We do not need a sense impression, as Hume had thought, of a "necessary connection." The necessary connection between the cause and the effect is a priori in our mind. We know, for example, that all heavy objects will fall in space and that two plus four always equals six. These ideas come from the mind. To say that only some objects fall in space or on Tuesdays two plus four equals nine are false statements. Thus, we do have knowledge about universal principles in both science and mathematics. A priori knowledge is always universally true.

A posteriori knowledge comes from our sense experience. This type of knowledge applies only to what we observe, and what we observe is always changing. Thus, a posteriori knowledge is never universally true. For example, you can see that a certain building is square or that the dog has shaggy hair. Yet, you cannot correctly conclude that *all* buildings are square or that *all* dogs have shaggy hair. A posteriori knowledge is not innate but based on our experience.

Two Kinds of Judgments

For Kant, we make a judgment when we connect a subject and a predicate. When you say, "The flower smells sweet," you are making a judgment. The mind understands the connection between the subject, "the flower," and the predicate, "smells sweet." Kant discovered that subjects and predicates connect to each other in two different ways. He called these judgments "analytic" and "synthetic." Analytic judgments are a priori, and synthetic judgments are a posteriori.

In analytic judgments, the predicate is already contained in the subject. For example, to say that all circles are round is an analytic judgment because the predicate, round, is contained in the subject, circle. The word *circle* means round. All bachelors are unmarried men is another example of an analytic judgment because the word *bachelor* means "unmarried man." Analytic judgments are always true. Circles are always round, and bachelors are always unmarried men. Because analytic judgments are a priori, they do not depend on sense experience.

Synthetic judgments add something new in the predicate that is not contained in the subject. When you say, "The orange is rotten," you join two separate ideas because the idea orange does not contain the idea of rotten. If you say, "The bachelor is on a holiday," the predicate, is on a holiday, tells something about the subject, the bachelor, that is not contained in it. Synthetic judgments are a posteriori because we discover by experience that the predicate adds information to the subject.

Synthetic A Priori Judgments

The key to Kant's philosophy is in the way he connected a priori judgments to a posteriori judgments. Scholars say this is how Kant put "philosophy back in the saddle." In a stroke of genius, Kant combined the two judgments into a third judgment that he called synthetic a priori. What seemed like a contradiction actually worked. Kant explained that we make synthetic a priori judgments in mathematics, science, and ethics. His argument for mathematical judgments as synthetic is as follows:

> *All mathematical judgments, without exception, are synthetic. . . .*
>
> We might, indeed, at first suppose that the proposition 7 + 5 = 12 is a merely analytic proposition, and follows by the principle of contradiction from the concept of a sum of 7 and 5. But if we look more closely we find that the concept of a sum of 7 and 5 contains nothing save the union of the two numbers into one, and in this no thought is being taken as to what that single number may be which combines both. The concept of 12 is by no means already thought in merely thinking this union of 7 and 5; and I may analyze my concept of such a possible sum as long as I please, still I

Kant lived in this house in Königsberg, East Prussia. His mother, Anna, took young Immanuel for walks in the nearby meadows and fields, teaching the curious child about the seasons, plants, and animals.

shall never find the 12 in it. We have to go outside these concepts, and call in the aid of the intuition [synthetic] which corresponds to one of them, or five fingers, for instance . . . adding to the concept of 7, unit by unit, the five given in intuition. For starting with the number 7, and for the concept of 5 calling in the aid of the fingers of my hand as intuition, I now add one by one to the number 7 the units which I previously took together to form the number 5, and with the aid of that figure see the number 12 come into being. That 5 should be added to 7, I have indeed already thought in the number 12. Arithmetical propositions are therefore always synthetic. This is still more evident if we take larger numbers. For it is then obvious that, however we might turn and twist our concepts, we could never, by the mere analysis of them, and without the aid of intuition, discover what is the sum. [25]

In mathematics, the judgment that 7 plus 5 equals 12 is a priori. It is always true. Seven plus 5 has to equal 12. At the same time, this judgment is synthetic because we cannot get the number 12 merely by analyzing the numbers 5 and 7. This is where experience comes into play: to make the synthesis of the concepts 7, 5, and plus. The plus sign (+) has different meanings when used in different circumstances. On top of a church, the plus sign could signify a cross, or tipped to the side, the plus sign could mean "railroad crossing." This also is true for the equals (=) sign. If the lines of the sign were extended, the symbol could look like a road, parallel lines, or a railroad track.

This means that we must first learn by experience the circumstances under which we use these signs. For example, when we see the plus (+) sign in mathematics, we have learned that that symbol means to add. That is synthetic. We know that 7 plus 5 always equals 12. That is a priori. We then have synthetic a priori, and that, for Kant, is how we get knowledge.

Another example Kant gave of synthetic a priori knowledge was using the statement, "The straight line between two points is the shortest." The statement is a priori because it is always true. Yet, the idea "straight" does not contain the idea "shortest." Thus, "shortest" is synthetic, depending on the situation. For example, to say that John is the shortest boy in his history class has nothing to do with a straight line.

> Just as little is any fundamental proposition of pure geometry analytic. That the straight line between two points is the shortest, is a synthetic proposition. For my concept of *straight* contains nothing of quantity, but only of quality. The concept of the shortest is wholly an addition, and cannot be derived, through any process of analysis, from the concept of the straight line. Intuition

[synthetic], therefore, must here be called in; only by its aid is the synthesis possible. [26]

Kant used this method to show that Hume was mistaken when he said there is no necessary connection between cause and effect. Without the law of cause and effect, this world would have no order. We would never know what to expect. If you threw a ball, you would never know if it would bounce, disappear in the clouds, or grow green feathers. What Kant calls into play is both a priori reason and experience. To Kant, it is synthetic a priori, his term for necessary connection. We know the law of gravity will bring the thrown ball back down to Earth. Thus, we know the law of cause and effect to be true.

God, Freedom, and Immortality

Hume had reached the conclusion that we cannot move beyond our own sense perceptions, but Kant found that the mind has the ability to organize the data of our sense experience, which means that knowledge does not end with sense experience. Yet, said Kant, there are limits to what we can know. When we ask about God or immortality, we reach well beyond the capacity of our mind. Why? Because knowledge begins with sense experience, and we have no sense experience of God or immortality. We can *think* about God, freedom, and immortality, but we could never *know* them. We can think them because these ideas are of the pure reason.

Moral Philosophy

Kant wanted to know if there are certain moral principles that all human beings must follow. He said we could not discover these principles by watching how people *do* behave because such observation does not tell us how people *ought* to behave.

Kant disagreed with Hume who said morals are a matter of sentiment. He agreed with the rationalists who said our moral abilities are innate in the reason. Everybody has practical reason, the capacity to know right from wrong. When we make moral judgments such as, "We ought to tell the truth," we are looking to a universal moral law. We know what our behavior should be. We know we ought to tell the truth and that we should not break promises.

Kant argued that all rational people are aware of having a moral duty to act in certain ways: When I say it is my duty to tell the truth, I am saying all rational people are a priori aware they ought to tell the truth. When I say I ought not lie, steal, cheat, or be disloyal, I am speaking for all rational people. Thus, when I consider what I must do, I am considering what all rational people must do. Morality is innate.

Goodwill

Just as the rules of logic and geometry are the same for everyone, so are moral rules the same for everyone. To act morally, said Kant, we must act with goodwill. Kant looked at morality not as obeying the rules of society, but as a duty based on goodwill. For Kant, "the goodwill is good not because of what it causes or accomplishes," but because "it is good in itself." The goodwill acts out of the highest motive without looking for certain results.

A good will is good not because of what it performs or [its] effect, not by it[s] aptness for the attainment of some proposed end, but simply by virtue of the volition, that is, it is good in itself, and considered by itself is to be esteemed much higher than all that can be brought about by it in favour of any inclination, nay, even of the sum-total of all inclinations. Even if it should happen

N. COPERNICUS.

London Publish'd as the Act directs April 20. 1802 by J.Wilkes

Kant compared his philosophy to the work of Polish astronomer
Nicholaus Copernicus, shown with a diagram illustrating his
revolutionary hypothesis that the Sun is the center of the universe. Kant
said, that, like Copernicus, he had gone outside the simple appearance
of the world to discover a new reality.

that, owing to special disfavour of fortune, or the nig-
gardly provision of a step-motherly nature, this will
should wholly lack power to accomplish its purpose, if
with its greatest efforts it should yet achieve nothing,
and there should remain only the good will (not, to be
sure, a mere wish, but the summoning of all means in
our power), then, like a jewel, it would still shine by its
own light, as a thing which has its whole value in itself.
Its usefulness or fruitlessness can neither add to nor
take away anything from this value. [27]

In other words, the good will acts out of a sense of duty,
avoiding any self-interest. The results of our actions are not the
importance of moral law. Our motive is what's important.

The moral law, said Kant, is a principle that I must obey.
I might be kind to people because I want them to like me, or
I might want to renege on my promise to return a book. Yet,
these wants are in my own self-interest, not based on moral law.
Moral law has nothing to do with self-interest. Moral law is a
duty. It is my duty to be kind to people and to keep my promises, based on goodwill.

Categorical Imperative

Kant insisted that duty comes to us in the form of a moral imperative: It is my moral duty to keep my promises; therefore,
I must keep my promises. A moral imperative is categorical
because it includes all rational people and applies to all situa-
tions. It is imperative because it is a moral principle on which
all rational people should act. This means we should act out of
moral duty and not look to the results of our actions. Kant's
Categorical Imperative states, "Act only on that maxim [prin-
ciple] whereby you can at the same time will [choose] that this
maxim become a universal law."

There remains nothing but the universal conformity of its actions to law in general, which alone is to serve the will as a principle, i.e., I am never to act otherwise than so *that I could also will that my maxim should become a universal law*. Here, now, it is the simple conformity to law in general, without assuming any particular law applicable to certain actions, that serves the will as its principle, and must so serve it, if duty is not to be a vain delusion and a chimerical notion. [28]

In other words, I should do my moral duty because it is my moral duty and for no other reason. For example, if I am about to tell a lie, I have to ask myself, "Would I want lying to become a universal law?" Kant believed that rational people would answer no.

Kant thought that, as rational beings, we wish others to treat us as ends in ourselves. When someone treats us as a means to their selfish end, or even tells us a lie, we become objects instead of persons.

Three Moral Postulates

Kant believed that it is essential for our morality to presuppose that we have an immortal soul, that God exists, and that we have a free will. These three postulates are based on faith. To postulate something is to assume something that cannot be proved, such as the immortal soul, that God exists, and that we have free will.

Immortality. Kant believed that we all strive for the supreme good, and we all strive to be happy. He said that striving for the supreme good implies an "endless progress" of the soul toward perfection. Because we could never be perfect in the present world, there must be a future world to perfect ourselves, and this means, said Kant, that immortality is true.

God.   Though we try our best to attain both happiness and the supreme good, we know we cannot do it by ourselves. None of us could have created the world, nor are we capable of telling nature to produce in us happiness and virtue. So, it is a moral necessity that we assume the existence of God. God desires that his creatures should be worthy of happiness. Because the Kingdom of God is within us, it is our moral duty to exhibit God in our lives. Although we can never prove God's existence, we should always see "[moral] duty as a divine command."

Freedom.   For Kant, we are acting freely only when we have goodwill and respect for moral law. We are never freer than when we conform to the moral law because we are acting with goodwill. Therefore, our duty to moral law depends entirely on our freedom to make moral choices.

LINKS TO HEGEL

Kant found that our reason is limited to knowledge of the physical world, but because we have the ability to think about the supernatural world and concepts such as God, freedom, and immortality, we must act on it. This discovery placed Kant among the great philosophers of the world. However, thinkers such as G.W.F. Hegel questioned Kant's conclusions.

Hegel was not a modest man. He claimed that he understood all of philosophy and history. In opposition to Kant, he thought that, if we could think about God, we could *know* God. Like Spinoza, Hegel thought that God and the universe were inseparable, but he had different ideas about how God worked. Ultimately, Hegel's thinking inspired enormous controversy over both the meaning of his philosophy as well as its adequacy.

5

IDEALISM AND MATERIALISM
Hegel and Marx

The philosophers have only interpreted
the world in various ways:
the point is to change it.
—Karl Marx

IDEALISM

The goal of philosophers throughout history was to search for the truth and to give an account of the universe and our place in it. Philosophers such as Socrates, Plato, and Descartes all agreed that truth is absolute, eternal, and unchanging. The universe is orderly and rational, they argued. By using our reason and our intuition, we could know our place in the scheme of things.

Other philosophers, such as the British empiricists, disagreed with the idea that we could know truth, the universe, or even our place in it. They found that human knowledge is limited to sense experience.

Kant mended the split between these two differing schools of thought, yet he found that our reason is limited. Even if we cannot know the absolute truth, he said, we yearn to know of God, freedom, and immortality, and so we must act on these ideals.

Like all philosophers who followed Kant, Georg Wilhelm Hegel was deeply influenced by him. Hegel believed if we can *think* about God, we could *know* God. We can know God because the "world spirit" is realizing itself through God, or Absolute Spirit via the human mind. Hegel's philosophy is known as idealism.

G.W.F. Hegel

Hegel's philosophy is mainly a method of understanding the process of history. He did not talk about eternal, unchanging truths because he saw everything in a constant state of change. He believed that history is like a running river, and so are human thoughts: They change depending upon the circumstances. For example, hundreds of years ago, slavery was acceptable, but today it is not. Not so long ago, horses were the mode of transportation, but today we have automobiles. Reason is always on the move, and human knowledge is constantly progressing.

Hegel's Life

Georg Wilhelm Friedrich Hegel (1770–1831) was born in Stuttgart, Germany, the son of a government official. Although the family was poor, they were close and affectionate. Hegel was born in an era of German intellectual giants such as composer Ludwig van Beethoven; philosopher and writer Johann Wolfgang Von Goethe, author of the masterpiece *Faust;* and the philosopher Immanuel Kant.

While a student at Tübingen University, Hegel read Plato and Aristotle, considering them to be the roots of all Western philosophy. After graduation, he showed a deep interest in the relationship between theology and philosophy and wrote essays revealing his insights. In one of his essays, Hegel compared the ethics of Socrates and Jesus, finding Socrates's moral teachings superior to those of the New Testament.

G.W.F. Hegel believed that God desires both to manifest himself and to know himself. Part of his essence is to become real in material things, people, and in the process of change and history. To Hegel, God is present in the real world, acting through humans.

Hegel was 19 years old when the French Revolution began. At that time, the starving lower classes in France rose up against the French aristocracy, sending shock waves of social and political upheaval across Europe. Hegel welcomed the revolution as a new age of freedom.

In 1799, Hegel's father died, leaving him enough money to quit tutoring and lecture without pay at the University of Jena. He also coedited a philosophy journal. During those years,

Hegel concentrated on writing his own philosophy. At that time, French emperor Napoleon Bonaparte's armies were on the march in a conquest of Europe. The same day that Hegel finished his first major work, *The Phenomenology of Mind*, Napoleon attacked Jena and closed the university. Soon after, Napoleon conquered Germany.

His inheritance gone, Hegel worked for a pro-Napoleon newspaper, and then as principal of a high school in Nürnberg. While there, he met and married Marie von Tucher, a woman half his age, with whom he had two sons. His philosophical works brought him invitations to teach from several universities. He joined the faculty at Heidelberg in 1816 and then accepted a position at the University of Berlin, where he remained until he fell ill with cholera. He died at age 61 at the height of his fame.

What is Real is Rational

Kant had said that we could never know the ultimate reality of God, freedom, and immortality, but we could and should think about ultimate reality. Hegel disagreed. The human mind is spirit just as God is Absolute Spirit. Therefore, we can know God. After all, he said, if we know there is Absolute Spirit, which is ultimate reality, then ultimate reality is knowable.

Reality is rational, and Hegel is noted for saying, "What is real is rational and what is rational is real." Plato, Descartes, Spinoza, and other philosophers also saw reality as rational. Plato saw the physical world as always changing, although true reality is permanent and never changing. Plato called the physical world an appearance of reality, making it less real. Hegel, however, argued that appearance *is* reality. For him, Absolute Spirit is the ultimate reality, and our world history is the "world spirit" gradually becoming conscious of itself through the human mind, which is also spirit. Humanity is moving toward greater rationality and freedom, he said. Absolute Spirit expresses itself through history via the dialectic process of "thesis, antithesis, and synthesis."

The Dialectic Process

For a thesis, or idea, to have any meaning, it must have an antithesis, or its opposite. In other words, we understand the concept of wet because we can relate to its opposite, dry. All ideas have their opposites. If we relate the idea to its opposite, we will discover a new truth: a synthesis, or a combination of thesis and antithesis. Imagine that you are having a discussion with someone of an opposing political party and tension begins to develop between your views. First, you think that the other person is totally wrong, then you begin to see that both of you could be partially right and partially wrong. This discovery leads to a synthesis. When you reach the synthesis, you present a new thesis, and the discussion continues. For Hegel, the world works in a similar fashion. Within the Absolute Spirit, everything is changing, which leads to a new thesis, antithesis, and synthesis. Absolute Spirit unfolds in the biological, social, and historical progression of the world. History is the story of Absolute Spirit evolving to greater and greater consciousness of itself through the "world spirit" via the human mind.

Nature, for Hegel, is Absolute Spirit in external form. Nature, which is based on sense experience, is the antithesis of the reason. Reason, he said, is logical (the thesis), nature is nonrational sense experience (the antithesis), and the Absolute Spirit unites the rational and the nonrational (the synthesis). Because nature must follow natural laws, Absolute Spirit cannot fully express itself, and, therefore, nature is unconscious of its own divinity.

Subjective and Objective Mind

According to Hegel, Absolute Spirit is the synthesis of reason and the senses, or the rational idea and nonrational nature.

The dialectic process moves through subjective spirit or mind (thesis); objective spirit, or mind (antithesis); and Absolute Spirit (synthesis).

At first, Absolute Spirit expresses itself in physical nature. Then, through our subjective nature, it begins to become conscious of itself in human beings. Hegel called this type of consciousness subjective spirit, or mind. It has three characteristics: (1) soul, (2) individual consciousness, and (3) intelligence. When the mind unites the soul and individual, it reaches the highest truth of the subjective spirit—the "free mind." We reach free mind when we learn to control our desires with the reason.

> This will to freedom is no longer an impulse that demands satisfaction, but the character—the mind's consciousness grown into something non-impulsive.
>
> [Freedom of the subjective mind is] a principle of mind and heart destined to develop into the objective phase, into legal, moral, religious and scientific actuality. [29]

When subjective spirit becomes conscious of the family, society, and the state, it becomes objective spirit. The objective spirit expresses itself when people interact. The subjective mind looks inward while the objective mind looks outward to the external world. Through the objective mind, we enter public life to create rules, institutions, and organizations. Just as the subjective mind has three states, so does the objective mind: (1) laws and contracts, (2) conscience, and (3) social morality.

At the first stage of laws and contracts, we create property systems, economic organizations, and class distinctions. We set up rights of ownership through buying and selling. The second stage takes us beyond physical possessions to responsibility. Conscience means that we must, as Kant said, have goodwill.

Recall that, for Kant, motive is the key and not the results of our actions. For Hegel, we must consider the results of our actions. We need to develop not only an inner conscience but also a social conscience. The third stage of social morality is the highest awareness of the objective mind, because here we see the importance of the family, social institutions, and the state.

> The family, as the immediate substantiality of mind, is specifically characterized by love, which is the mind's feeling of its own unity. Hence in a family, one's frame of mind is to have self-consciousness of one's individuality within this unity as the [ab]solute essence of oneself, with the result that one is in it not as an independent person but as a member. [30]

The State

For Hegel, the state is especially important. He said that, because the state is a living unity of individuals, it becomes the true individual. Hegel said the true state is the ethical whole and the realization of freedom: It is the "march of God through the world," according to Hegel. After watching Napoleon ride through Jena, Hegel said that he had seen Absolute Spirit on horseback.

> The state is the actuality of the ethical Idea. It is ethical mind *qua* [in the capacity of] the substantial will manifest and revealed to itself, in knowing and thinking itself, accomplishing what it knows and in so far as it knows it. The state exists immediately in custom, immediately in individual self-consciousness, knowledge, and activity, which self-conscious in virtue of its sentiment towards the state, finds in the state, as its essence and the end and product of its activity, its substantive freedom. [31]

Hegel called the state a rational and self-conscious force expressing universal reason, in which the citizens of a society lose their independence in the unity of the state.

World History

Hegel's philosophy is highly complex. It is a huge system that moves through history like a giant snowball gathering more and more snow as it goes. Hegel saw history as humanity's path to self-discovery and the history of the world as the history of nations. Each nation expresses a "national spirit" of its own collective consciousness. The conflict between national spirits is the dialectical process in history. That is why we see the rise and fall of nations.

The history of a single world-historical nation contains (a) the development of its principle from its latent embryonic

The Battle of Jena was fought between the armies of Napoleon Bonaparte and Prussia in October 1806. Hegel believed that Napoleon embodied the hero of his age, driving toward the self-realization of God in history.

stage until it blossoms into the self-conscious freedom of ethical life and presses in upon world history; and (b) the period of its decline and fall, since it is its decline and fall that signalizes the emergence in it of a higher principle as the pure negative of its own. When this happens, mind passes over into the new principle and so marks out another nation for world-historical significance. [32]

Hegel believed that, under the influence of Christianity, the Germanic peoples developed the highest rational insight: that humans are free. The highest freedom of nations occurs when we act according to the universal rational will of the Absolute Spirit.

Art, Religion, Philosophy

Hegel thought the highest expression of reality was Absolute Spirit. Our knowledge of Absolute Spirit is actually Absolute Spirit knowing itself through humanity's spirit. For Hegel, the process goes through three stages: from art to religion, and finally to philosophy.

As everything else, Hegel saw art as a dialectic development of Absolute Spirit: (1) symbolic; (2) classical; and (3) romantic. Symbolic art is vague in its form of expression. It suggests a meaning without adequately expressing it. Classical art harmonizes form and spirit equally. Romantic art is the highest expression of art because spirit triumphs over form. As the world progresses, so does its art.

Religion also has developed through three stages of Absolute Spirit: (1) religions of nature; (2) religions of spiritual individuality; and (3) absolute religion. In religions of nature, humans use worship to control nature through magic. Religions of spiritual individuality provide the cultural background of Christianity, the highest religion of the Absolute Spirit. According to Hegel, Christ's death expressed the alienation between the finite (thesis) and the infinite (antithesis), and their ultimate union (synthesis). Without this doctrine, people would still view God as "other than" and beyond the world.

In philosophy, the artist's external sensuous vision (thesis) and the religious mystic's internal vision (antithesis) unite in thought (synthesis). Philosophy is like the mirror of the Absolute Spirit because the history of philosophy is the dialectical process of Absolute Spirit's self-consciousness in the human mind.

MATERIALISM

The era of the huge philosophical systems seems to have ended with Hegel. After him, philosophy took a new direction, and in place of speculation, we find philosophies of action. This is what Karl Marx meant when he said, "The philosophers have only interpreted the world differently: the point is to change it."

For Marx, nothing beyond this world even exists. Ideas of God and immortality are childish ideas. Like psychoanalyst Sigmund Freud, Marx thought that as children we see our father as God, and as we grow up and realize our own father is not perfect, we look for a perfect father in heaven. Yet, there is no heaven and there is no God. Marx called God the "opiate of the people." There is no God, but we try to convince ourselves there is because we don't want to take responsibility for our lives.

Although Marx rejected Hegel's notion of Absolute Spirit, he liked his idea of one reality. Reality for Marx is the connection between our consciousness and our culture. He also agreed with Hegel that history is a process of change but change that occurs in matter and not in spirit. It has been said, "Marx stood Hegel on his head." Marx's philosophy is known as dialectical materialism.

Karl Marx

As a materialist arguing that matter is reality, Marx agreed with Hegel that the dialectical process takes place in nature and in

history. He disagreed with Hegel's idealism that the dialectic is the process of the Absolute Spirit. Hegel's pyramid is upside down, said Marx, and he wanted to turn it over on its "material base." That is why philosophers say Marx turned Hegel on his head.

What makes us human, said Marx, is that we produce. Through productive activities such as fishing, farming, and building, we develop a society that in turn shapes us. Hegel had said that spirit determines our existence. Marx took the opposite view:

> The mode of production of material life conditions the general process of social, political, and intellectual life. It is not the consciousness of men that determines their existence, but their social existence that determines their consciousness. [33]

Marx's Life

Karl Marx (1818–1883), the third of nine children, was born in Trier, Germany. His parents were Jewish, but to protect his father's job as a government lawyer, they changed their name from Levi to Marx and converted to Protestant Christianity.

Karl was highly intelligent and was influenced by his father's intelligence and his concern for others. Another influence in his life was a neighbor and well-known government official, Ludwig von Westphalen, who later became his father-in-law. Westphalen introduced him to the works of the Greek poets as well as to those of Dante and Shakespeare.

At age 17, Marx enrolled in the University of Bonn to study law. Law took a backseat to his partying, however, and to the love letters he wrote to Jenny von Westphalen. When his father discovered what was going on, he transferred Marx to the University of Berlin. There, Marx was so impressed with Hegel that he gave up law to study philosophy. He also became a member of the young radical Hegelians. As a group, these students searched for a new understanding of human nature and the world.

At 23, Marx received his doctoral degree from the University of Jena, but after graduation, no university would hire him. The young Hegelians had become radical leftists, and they publicly criticized the New Testament Gospels. About this time, Marx's father died, leaving only enough money to support Marx's mother and family. Marx was not only on his own but out of a job.

Finally, a Hegelian publisher of a liberal newspaper, the *Rhenish Gazette*, based in Cologne, Germany, hired Marx as editor. His editorials, however, caused such uproars that the government suppressed the paper and Marx was again out of a job. He went to Paris, found a job as coeditor of a German-French journal, and married Jenny. Yet, the journal soon closed, and he was again jobless. For a short period, a settlement from the shareholders of the *Rhenish Gazette* kept Marx and Jenny financially secure.

After reading an article by German philosopher and anthropologist Ludwig Feuerbach, Marx's own philosophy began to shift to materialism. Feuerbach argued that history is the result of economic circumstances that influence people's minds and actions, not the struggle of Absolute Spirit to realize itself. This view excited Marx because it explained human thinking and behavior. Human beings were not the product of God's creation—God was the product of human creation. With his new ideas, Marx combined Hegel's dialectic view of history and Feuerbach's view of the material order.

While in Paris, Marx met German philosopher and social scientist Friedrich Engels, who would become his friend, collaborator, and financial backer. Together, Marx and Engels wrote *The Holy Family* in which they criticized many of their fellow leftists. During his year in Paris, Marx was politically

active among the German communists. They asked Marx to write an easy-to-read pamphlet explaining their views. He did, and this pamphlet became the famous *Communist Manifesto*. Furious with his communist involvement, the French government expelled him from the country.

For the next 20 years, Marx and his family lived in London. Because he mismanaged funds, they lived in poverty, and for the rest of his life, most of his income consisted of gifts from Engels. Isolating himself to study and write, Marx worked long hours to produce his philosophy. In his last work, *Das Kapital*, he looked forward to a revolution that would crush capitalism.

During his final years, Marx developed a liver disorder. His wife, Jenny, became ill and his six-year-old son died. In 1881, Jenny died, and Marx's oldest daughter died in 1883. Two years later, Marx died at age 65.

Dialectical Materialism

Hegel had argued that Absolute Spirit is the driving force of the world. Marx took exactly the opposite view, claiming that the driving force of the world is economics, not spirit. For Marx, the material factors in society, such as the economy and production, determine the way we think and behave.

Using Hegel's thesis, antithesis, and synthesis method, Marx proposed "five epochs of history": (1) the primitive, or communal; (2) slave; (3) feudal; (4) capitalist; and (5) socialist or communist. The tension between the bourgeoisie, or ruling class, and the proletariat, or oppressed working class, creates the conflict between the rulers and the exploited. The basis for each historical epoch, said Marx, is its economic structure (its production).

> That in every historical epoch, the prevailing mode
> of economic production and exchange, and the social

Karl Marx argued that religion was a force that stopped society from changing because the ruling class used it to keep the working class under control. By focusing on the joys in the afterlife and distracting itself from conditions in the present life, the working class used religion to comfort itself in its oppressed state.

organization necessarily following from it, from the basis upon which is built up, and from which alone can be explained, the political and intellectual history of that epoch; that consequently the whole history of mankind… has been a history of class struggles, contests between exploiting and exploited, ruling and oppressed classes; that the history of these class struggles forms a series of evolutions in which a state has been reached where the exploited and oppressed class—the proletariat—cannot attain its emancipation from the sway of the exploiting and ruling class—the bourgeoisie—without at the same time, and once and for all, emancipating society at large from all exploitation, oppression, class distinctions and class struggles. [34]

Production. According to Marx, we are social animals with physical needs, and we satisfy those needs by the "means of production." The production of goods such as clothes, computers, television, and food products, determines the type of political, social, and religious life of every society in history. Because the needs of each society differ, people in those societies think differently. A cotton farmer will have different production needs than a hotel owner, and each will think according to his or her needs. Economic production shapes our ideas.

For Marx, the economic structure controls the outlook of every human being in society. We might think our ideas control the economy, but it is actually economic production that shapes our ideas.

Based on his idea of the dialectic, the forces of production develop until they conflict with existing social relationships. Marx believed, for example, that religion or belief in God is an opiate, or drug, of the people. Once we straighten out our society by evolving from capitalism to communism, the need for such a God in the sky will simply vanish.

Man makes religion; religion does not make man. "Religion is indeed man's self-consciousness and self-awareness so long as he has not found himself or has lost himself again." [35]

Alienation.   Hegel had argued that Absolute Spirit produced nature out of itself, which then caused a thesis/antithesis relationship between humans and nature. Marx saw alienation differently. For him, alienation is the separation of individual workers from the product of their labor. In mankind's early history, when primitive people lived in tribes, everyone helped to produce what the community needed. There was no separation between an individual and the product of his labor.

As communities evolved and grew larger, so did production needs, and a division of labor began. When the basket weaver started exchanging baskets for products made by other people, the basket became an object of trade. Individuals became known as specialists in their fields—basket weaver, farmer, baker, and barber. Workers became alienated from the products of their labor. When workers only make products for market value, oppression is born.

Capitalism, said Marx, is the major oppressor. In a capitalist society, the workers are slaves for another social class, transferring their labor and their lives to the capitalist. In return, they receive meager wages. This dehumanizes workers into beasts of burden. During the early part of the Industrial Revolution, for example, there was no solidarity among workers. Workers might work 12 hours a day in a freezing cold factory. They competed against each other for jobs. Such competition not only alienated workers from their product and their employer but also from each other.

> It is true that labor produces for the rich wonderful things—but for the worker it produces privation. It produces palaces—but for the worker, hovels. It produces beauty—but for the worker, deformity. It replaces labor by machines, but it throws a section of the workers back to a barbarous type of labor, and it turns the other

workers into machines. It produces intelligence—but for the worker stupidity, cretinism. [36]

Alienated labor leads to ownership, private property, and human perversion. The rich got richer, the poor got poorer. Such exploitation infuriated Marx. He said the need for money becomes the lust for money, and greed keeps the process alive. Devotion to money becomes a kind of religion.

Communism

Capitalism, insisted Marx, would continue until "all workers of the world unite" and become a revolutionary class. Capitalism cannot survive the socialization of production, and capitalism will fail. Overproduction will result in economic crises. Then, when the working class wakes up to its conditions, it will overthrow capitalism. Communism will follow in its wake.

Communism is a classless society made up of workers guided by the communist motto, "From each according to his abilities, to each according to his needs!" In the classless society, the economic struggle between the capitalist and working classes will stop as all merge into the working class. There will be no private property:

> You are horrified at our intending to do away with private property. But in your existing society, private property is already done away with for nine-tenths of the population; its existence for the few is solely due to its non-existence in the hands of those nine-tenths. You reproach us, therefore, with intending to do away with a form of property, the necessary condition for whose existence is, the non-existence of any property for the immense majority of society.

In one word, you reproach us with intending to do away with your property. Precisely so; that is just what we intend. . . .

Communism deprives no man of the power to appropriate the products of society; all that it does is to deprive him of the power to subjugate the labour of others by means of such appropriation. [37]

A classless society would replace the proletariat, and the people would own the means of production. Labor would belong to the workers themselves, and capitalism would come to an end. Marx viewed communism as a classless and godless society.

Marx's philosophy later influenced the Russian revolutionary Vladimir Ilich Lenin and Chinese leader Mao Tse-Tung who both agreed there could be no progress without physical violence. Although Marx thought his philosophy would bring an end to capitalism, it had less effect on Western capitalism than on underdeveloped countries in Asia, Africa, and Latin America.

SUMMARY AND LINKS TO POSTMODERN AND CONTEMPORARY PHILOSOPHY

Medieval and modern philosophy began with early Christian philosophers: Augustine and Aquinas, Jewish philosopher Maimonides, and Muslim philosopher Avicenna. These philosophers were also theologians, studying God. The main issues concerning them were God, the story of creation, and our human relationship with both. One of the big debates during the medieval ages was between faith and reason.

Is God a divine mystery that we can only perceive through faith, or because God endowed human beings with rational minds did he intend humans to use reason to know him?

Closing the medieval ages were the Renaissance, the Protestant Reformation, and the rise of science. The Renaissance ushered in a new view of humanity. Human beings were no longer considered lowly and sinful creatures. The Reformation began with Martin Luther, who protested the practices of the Roman Catholic Church and gave birth to the Protestant religion.

Before the rise of science, Christians believed that God created humankind in his image, and Earth was the center of the universe. Soon, scientists such as Copernicus and Galileo discovered that it was not the Sun that moved around Earth, but that Earth and other planets revolved around the Sun. Newton formulated the law of gravity. Thomas Hobbes viewed humankind as purely material beings who needed a "social contract" to survive in society.

The Continental rationalists, Descartes, Spinoza, and Leibnez, thought science was too limited. They believed that universal truths—such as that there is a God and that the universe is rational—exist, and that by using reason they could know these truths. These philosophers accepted, almost without question, that the rational mind could produce certain knowledge about science and human nature.

The British empiricists, Locke, Berkeley, and Hume, challenged the idea that by using the rational mind we could know the meaning of human existence and the universe. All we can know, they said, is what we experience with our five senses, and those senses can never give us absolute certainty of anything.

Kant sought to answer the British empiricists by analyzing the capacity of reason. His philosophy was one of the important turning points in Western philosophy.

The idealist Hegel claimed that the rational mind can know the truth of God and immortality, while the materialist Marx argued that our knowledge is limited to facts of the material world.

The next wave of thinking would usher in the postmodern and contemporary eras of philosophy. The first of these philosophers were utilitarians. These philosophers rejected the idealism of Hegel and the dialectical materialism of Marx because they believed that the British empiricists were right. The utilitarians wanted to improve the methods of empiricism, especially in the field of ethics. According to utilitarians, moral actions are those that produce the greatest happiness for the greatest number of people. The basis for utilitarian philosophy is the "greatest happiness principle." The coming of the Industrial Revolution would set the stage for these new thinkers.

NOTES

CHAPTER 1

1. Wallace I. Matson, *A New History of Philosophy*. Vol. I. San Diego: Harcourt Brace Jovanovich, 1987, p.193.
2. Augustine, *Confessions*, Bk. XIII, Ch. 12:29, trans. by Edward Bouverie Pusey, in *Great Books of the Western World*. Vol. 18. Chicago: Encyclopedia Britannica, 1952, p. 61.
3. Ibid., Bk. I, Ch. 2, p. 1.
4. Augustine, *City of God*, Bk. XXII, Ch. 1, trans. by Marcus Dods, in *Great Books of the Western World*. Vol. 18. Chicago: Encyclopedia Britannica, 1952, p. 587.
5. Ibid., Bk. XXII, Ch. 22, pp. 606–607, 608.
6. Ibid., Vol. XIV, Ch. 28, p. 397.
7. Moses Maimonides, *Guide for the Perplexed*, ed. by Forrest E. Baird and Walter Kaufman, *Medieval Philosophy*, in *Philosophical Classics*, 2nd ed. Vol. II. New Jersey: Prentice Hall, 1997, pp. 240–241.
8. Martyn Oliver, *History of Philosophy*. Great Britain: Barnes & Noble, in arrangement with Hamlyn, 1998, p. 50.
9. W.T. Jones, *The Medieval Mind: A History of Western Philosophy*. Vol. II. New York: Harcourt, Brace & World, 1969, p. 209.

CHAPTER 2

10. Henry Wace and C.A. Buchein, *Luther's Primary Work*. Philadelphia: Luther Publishing Society, 188, p. 53.

11. L. Stephen, *Hobbes*. London: Macmillan, 1904, pp. 17–18.
12. Renè Descartes, "Meditations on First Philosophy," trans. by E.S. Haldane and G.R.T. Ross, in *The Philosophical Works of Descartes*. London: Cambridge University Press, 1931, pp. 165–166.
13. Ibid., Vol. I., pp. 192, 196, and from "The Passion of the Soul," in *Works*, op.cit. Vol. I, pp. 345–46.
14. Walter Kaufman and Forrest E. Baird, *From Plato to Nietzsche*. New Jersey: Prentice Hall, 1994, p. 477.
15. Robert Willis, *Benedict de Spinoza*. London: Trübner & Company, 1870, pp. 35–36. Quoted in Wallace I. Matson, *A New History of Philosophy*. Vol.II. New York: Harcourt Brace Jovanovich, 1987.
16. Spinoza, *Ethics and on the Improvement of the Understanding*, Prop. XLII, Note, ed. by James Gutmann. New York: Hafner Publishing, 1949, p. 242.
17. Ibid., Prop. XlII, appendix, p. 280.
18. Gottfried Wilhelm Leibniz, *Monadology*, trans. by P.P. Wiener, in *Leibniz: Selections*. New York: Scribners, 1951, pp. 533–534.

CHAPTER 3

19. John Locke, *An Essay Concerning Human Understanding*, Bk. II. Ch. 1, 2. Chicago: *Great Books of the Western World*, University of Chicago

Press, Encyclopedia Britannica, 1952, p. 121.

20. Ibid., Bk. II, Chap. 21, 35, p. 186.

21. John Locke, *An Essay Concerning Human Understanding*, ed. by H.C. Fraser. Oxford: Clarendon Press, 1894, in W.T. Jones, *A History of Western Philosophy* 2nd ed., Vol. III. New York: Harcourt Brace Jovanovich, 1969, pp. 262–264.

22. David Hume, *An Enquiry Concerning the Human Understanding*, Sec. II, 13. Chicago: *Great Books of the Western World*, University of Chicago Press, Enclyclopedia Britannica, 1952, pp. 455–456.

23. Ibid., p. 456.

24. David Hume, *A Treatise of Human Nature*, ed. by L.A. Selby-Brigge, Sec. 6. Oxford: Oxford University Press, 1888.

CHAPTER 4

25. Immanuel Kant, *Critique of Pure Reason*, trans. by N. Kemp Smith. London: Macmillan, 1929, pp. 14–15.

26. Ibid., p. 16.

27. Immanuel Kant, *Fundamental Principles of the Metaphysics of Morals*, trans. by T.K. Abbott, Sec. I. London: Longmans & Green, 1927, p. 10.

28. Ibid., Sec. I, p. 18.

CHAPTER 5

29. G.W.F. Hegel, *The Phenomenology of Mind*, 2nd ed., trans. by T.B. Baillie, Sec. 482. London: Sonnenschien, 1931.

30. G.W.F. Hegel, *Philosophy of Right*, trans. by T. M. Knox, Subsec. 1, Sec. 158. Chicago: University of Chicago Press, *Great Books of the Western World*, Encyclopedia Britannica, 1952, p. 58.

31. Ibid., Subsec. III, Sec. 257, p. 80.

32. Ibid., Sec. 347, p. 111.

33. Richard Schmitt, *Introduction to Marx and Engels*. Boulder, Colo: Westview Press, 1987, pp. 7–8.

34. Karl Marx and Friedrich Engels, *Manifesto of the Communist Party*, trans. by Samuel Moore, Preface. Chicago: Encyclopedia Britannica, 1952, p. 416.

35. Karl Marx, "Contribution to the Critique of Hegel's Philosophy of Right," in *Early Writings*, trans. by T.B. Bottomore. London: C.A. Watts, 1963, p. 43.

36. *The Economic and Philosophic Manuscripts of 1844*, ed. by Dirk J. Struik. New York: International Publishers, 1964, p. 110.

37. *Manifesto of the Communist Party*, op. cit., p. 426.

GLOSSARY

Absolute Spirit　The ultimate reality, God, in Hegel's philosophy.

amoral　No inner sense of right and wrong; without morals.

analytic statements　For Kant, statements that are necessarily true because the predicate is already contained in the subject.

a posteriori　Knowledge based on sense experience.

a priori　Innate ideas the reason can know without using the senses.

cause　That which has the power to produce change in another thing.

canonize　To declare someone an officially recognized saint.

categorical imperative　Kant's moral law based on duty and goodwill that asks us to act in such a way that our action would become a universal law.

deduction　Using reason to arrive at a truth by a step-by-step process.

dialectic process or materialism　For Hegel, a process using thesis and antithesis to arrive at a synthesis. For Marx, a clash of material forces producing dynamic change.

emanate　In philosophical thought, an "overflowing," or creating process.

empiricism　The view that all knowledge of facts arises from sense experience.

Forms　In Plato's view, Forms are the ideal patterns beyond space/time. Forms are the true reality, immaterial, and eternal.

free will　The view that human beings have free and independent choice.

Hellenistic   The period of Greek civilization following the death of Alexander the Great (300–100 B.C.)

heresy   The rejection of an article of faith by a baptized member of the Roman Catholic Church.

heretic   A baptized Roman Catholic who rejects an article of faith.

hypothesis   A theory that explains the results of some testing.

idealism   The philosophical theory that reality consists of ideas, spirit, mind, or thought.

immoral   Morally wrong; bad or not right.

immortality   Everlasting soul or spirit.

Index of Forbidden Books   A list of publications that the Catholic Church censored for being a danger to itself and the faith of its members.

innate ideas   Ideas present in the mind at birth that rational human beings can know independently of sense experience.

intuition   Direct and clear insights into basic truths.

logic   The laws of thought or reason.

Logos   Meaning "word or reason." The ordering principle of the world.

materialism   The belief that everything is composed of matter and can be explained by physical laws.

Messiah   The promised savior of the Jewish people.

metaphysics   The field of philosophy concerned with the ultimate nature of reality; speculation of things beyond the physical world.

mind–body problem   In Descartes, the problem of how the relationship between the spiritual mind and the physical body takes place in human nature.

mode   In Spinoza's philosophy, modes are expressions, forms, or appearances of God's attributes.

monad   In Leibniz's philosophy, monads are the soul-like basic elements of the universe.

monastic   Resembling the secluded or serene life in a monastery.

moral   Proper conduct.

mortal sin   According to the Roman Catholic Church, mortal sins harm the soul, and are unpardonable.

mystic   One who experiences an intimate union of the soul with God; one who understands the mysteries of life.

objective   Considering the object independently of the person; an impartial view.

original sin   According to Christianity, an inclination toward evil in all human beings inherited from the sin of Adam and Eve.

pantheism   The view that God is in the world and the world is in God.

perception   The sensory faculty by which we obtain knowledge about the world.

phenomenal world   In Kant's philosophy, the world of our sense experience.

polytheism   The belief in more than one God or in many gods.

pope   The head of the Roman Catholic Church.

purgatory   A Roman Catholic belief in a state following death in which souls are purified of sins to make them ready for heaven.

rabbi   A Jewish scholar or teacher.

rationalism   The view that our knowledge is derived from the reason and not from sense experience.

reincarnation   The passing of the immortal soul through many cycles of birth, death, and rebirth.

revelation   Something that is revealed by God to humans.

Semitic   Relating to the peoples from southwestern Asia including the Hebrews and Arabs.

skeptic   A person who questions our ability to have knowledge of reality.

subjective   Concerning the person, the individual; the opposite of objective.

synagogue   A Jewish house of worship, religious instruction, and community center.

synthetic statements   For Kant, in synthetic statements the predicate is not contained in the subject, but adds something to the subject.

Talmud   A written collection of Jewish law and tradition.

tabula rasa   Latin for "blank tablet," Locke's idea of the human mind at birth.

theology   The study of God and God's relation to the universe.

venial sin   Pardonable by the Roman Catholic Church because we can make amends.

virtue   A morally excellent quality of character.

BIBLIOGRAPHY

Augustine. *City of God*, trans. by Marcus Dods, *Great Books of the Western World*, Vol. 18. Chicago: Encyclopedia Britannica, 1952.

———. *Confessions*, trans. by Edward Bouverie Pusey, *Great Books of the Western World*, Vol. 18. Chicago: Encyclopedia Britannica, 1952.

Descartes, René. "Meditations on First Philosophy," in *The Philosophical Works of Descartes*, trans. by E.S. Haldane and G.R.T Ross. London: Cambridge University Press, 1931.

———. "The Passion of the Soul," in *The Philosophical Works of Descartes*, trans. by E.S. Haldane and G.R.T. Ross. London: Cambridge University Press, 1931.

The Economic and Philosophic Manuscripts of 1844. Edited by Dirk J. Struik. New York: International Publishers, 1964.

Hegel, G.W.F. *The Phenomenology of Mind*, 2nd ed., ed. by T.B. Baillie. London: Sonnenschien, 1931.

———. *Philosophy of Right*, trans. by T. M. Knox. Chicago: University of Chicago Press, *Great Books of the Western World*, Encyclopedia Britannica, 1952.

Hume, David. *A Treatise of Human Nature*, ed. by L.A. Selby-Brigge. Oxford: Oxford University Press, 1888.

———. *An Enquiry Concerning the Human Understanding*. Chicago: *Great Books of the Western World*, University of Chicago Press, Encyclopedia Britannica, 1952.

Kant, Immanuel. *Critique of Pure Reason*, trans. by N. Kemp Smith. London: Macmillan, 1929.

———. *Fundamental Principles of the Metaphysics of Morals*, trans. by T.K. Abbott. London: Longmans & Green, 1927.

Kaufman, Walter, and Forrest E. Baird. *From Plato to Nietzsche*. New Jersey: Prentice Hall, 1994.

Leibniz, Gottfried Wilhelm. *Monandology*, trans. by P.P. Weiner, in *Leibniz: Selections*. New York: Scribners, 1951.

Locke, John. *An Essay Concerning Human Understanding*, Bk. II, Ch. 1, 2. Chicago: University of Chicago Press, Encyclopedia Britannica, 1952.

————. *An Essay Concerning Human Understanding*, ed. by H.C. Fraser. Oxford: Clarendon Press, 1894, in W.T. Jones, *A History of Western Philosophy*, 2nd ed., Vol. III. New York: Harcourt Brace Jovanovich Publishers, 1969.

Maimonides, Moses. *Guide for the Perplexed*, ed. by Forrest E. Baird and Walter Kaufman, *Medieval Philosophy*, in *Philosophical Classics*, 2nd ed., Vol. II. New Jersey: Prentice Hall, 1997.

Marx, Karl. "Contribution to the Critique of Hegel's Philosophy of Right," in *Karl Marx: Early Writings*, trans. by T.B. Bottomore. London: C.A. Watts, 1963.

Marx, Karl, and Friedrich Engels. *Manifesto of the Communist Party*, trans. by Samuel Moore. Chicago: Encyclopedia Britannica, 1952.

Matson, Wallace I. *A New History of Philosophy*, Vol. I. San Diego: Harcourt Brace Jovanovich, 1987.

————. *A New History of Philosophy*, Vol. II. New York: Harcourt Brace Jovanovich, 1987.

Oliver, Martyn. *History of Philosophy*. Great Britain: Barnes & Noble, in arrangement with Hamlyn, 1998.

Schmitt, Richard. *Introduction to Marx and Engels*. Boulder, Colo: Westview Press, 1987.

Spinoza, Benedict de. *Ethics and on the Improvement of the Understanding*, ed. by James Gutmann. New York: Hafner Publishing, 1949.

Stephen, L. *Hobbes*. London: Macmillan, 1904.

Wace, Henry, and C.A. Buchein. *Luther's Primary Works*. Philadelphia: Luther Publishing Society, 1885.

Willis, Robert. *Benedict de Spinoza*. London: Trübner & Company, 1870.

FURTHER READING

BOOKS

Bahr, Ann Marie B. *Christianity*. Philadelphia: Chelsea House, 2004.

Carver, Terrell. *The Cambridge Companion to Marx*. Cambridge: Cambridge University Press, 2006.

Fox, Michael Allen. *The Accessible Hegel*. Amherst, NY: Humanity Books, 2005.

Grayling, A.C. *Descartes: The Life and Times of a Genius*. New York: Walker & Company, 2006.

Jolley, N. *Leibniz*. Oxford: Routledge, 2005.

Marty, Martin E. *Martin Luther*. New York: Viking, 2004.

Mossner, Ernest Campbell. *The Life of David Hume*. Oxford: Oxford University Press, 2001.

Nasr, Seyyed Hossein. *Islam: Religion, History, and Civilization*. San Francisco: Harper San Francisco, 2002.

Nuland, Sherwin B. *Maimonides*. New York: Schocken Publishing, 2005.

Plum, J.H. *The Italian Renaissance*. Boston: Mariner Books, 2001.

Van Nieuwenhove, Rik, and Joseph Wawrykow, eds. *The Theology of Thomas Aquinas*. Notre Dame, IN: University of Notre Dame Press, 2005.

Woolhouse, Roger. *Locke: A Biography*. Cambridge, UK: Cambridge University Press, 2007.

WEB SITES

history.hanover.edu/early/prot.html

plato.stanford.edu/entries/hegel/

www.bbc.co.uk/religion/religions/christianity/history/

www.friesian.com/kant.htm

www.historyguide.org/intellect/marx.html

www.iep.utm.edu/

www.mrdowling.com/704renaissance.html

www.muslimphilosophy.com/

www.philosophyprofessor.com/philosophies/british-empiricists.php

www.philosophyprofessor.com/philosophies/continental-rationalists
.php

PICTURE CREDITS

INDEX

A

a posteriori knowledge, 89
a priori knowledge, 88–89
Absolute Spirit, 102–104, 109, 110, 114
Active Intellect, 26
Adam and Eve, 8, 19
Albertus Magnus (Albert the Great), 30
alienation, 114–115
Allah. *See* God
Ambrose, 12, 16
animals as machines (Descartes), 54
antithesis, 103
Aquinas. *See* Thomas Aquinas
Aristotle, 20, 25, 29
art, 107
Ashley, Lord, 65, 66
astronomy, 42–43
atomists, 79
Augustine
  overview, 15
  church history and, 12
  City of God and City of the
    World, 22–23
  creation, 17–18
  God, 17
  Greek philosophy and, 14–15
  history, view of, 23
  life of, 15–16
  love, 7, 20–22
  Luther and, 41
  moral philosophy, 18–22
Averroes, 25
Avicenna, 25–26

B

Berkeley, Bishop George
  overview, 70
  life of, 70–72
  "to be is to be perceived," 72–74
Bible, 7–8, 11, 41
body and mind, 52–53, 76
Boyle, Robert, 43
British empiricists. *See* empiricism
Bruno, Giordano, 37

C

The Canon of Medicine (Avicenna), 25
capitalism, 114–115
Cartesian method, 48–49
categorical imperative, 96–97
Catholicism. *See* Roman Catholic
  Church
cause, efficient, 32
cause, First, 26, 32
cause and effect, 78–79, 83, 93
celibacy, 13
Charlemagne, 23–24
Christianity. *See also* Roman Catholic
  Church
  Hegel on, 107–108
  high point for, 28–29
  philosophy and early
    Christianity, 13–15
  Protestant Reformation, 41–42
  rise of, 11–13
  roots of, 7–11
Christina, Queen of Sweden, 47
church, brief history of, 12–13
The City of God (Augustine), 22–23
civil law, 69
class struggles, 112–113
communism, 111, 115–116
Communist Manifesto (Marx and
  Engels), 111
conscience, 104
contemporary philosophy, 118

ABOUT THE AUTHOR

JOAN A. PRICE has a Ph.D. in philosophy from Arizona State University. She was a philosophy professor at Mesa Community College for 30 years and cofounder of the Department of Religious Studies. She was chairperson of the Department of Philosophy and Religious Studies for five years and is presently professor emeritus of philosophy at Mesa Community College.

Joan has written dozens of magazine and journal articles and is the author of *Truth is a Bright Star: A Hopi Adventure*, translated into Japanese and Korean; *Hawk in the Wind*; *Medicine Man*; *J.K. Rowling: A Biography*; and *Great Religious Leaders* for middle-grade and young adult readers. Her adult books include *Introduction to Sri Aurobindo's Philosophy*; *Philosophy Through the Ages*, a textbook for college students; and *Climbing the Spiritual Ladder*.

She is an animal lover with three dogs and several flocks of wild geese and ducks that camp on the lake by her house for daily handouts. She lives in Scottsdale, Arizona.